P9-BYW-399

FORT WORTH PUBLIC LIBRARY

3 1668 03464 1610

FORT WORTH

PUBLIC LIBRARY

IN MEMORY OF

GEORGE ANSLEY

July 2006

635.965 HEFFERNAN 2006
Heffernan, Cecelia
Houseplants A to Z

Wedgwood

WEDGWOOD BRANCH

SEP 0 1 2006

Cecelia Heffernan
Photography by T. K. Hill
Artisan · New York

houseplants A to Z

Buying

Growing

Arranging

Contents

Introduction: Knowing Plants

Growing plants is about discovering nature, experimenting, and learning. It is uniquely rewarding to watch plants grow and thrive in our own garden, to create a garden and bring it to life with different types of plants. Our gardens give us a tranquil place to reflect and escape from the everyday.

Growing houseplants allows us to bring some of this same joy from outside to inside. Plants give a touch of nature to a room, a home, or any setting—from a splash of color and the scent of exotic flowering plants to the cooling shades of green and the various shapes, patterns, forms, and textures of the foliage plants.

Houseplants A to Z will show you how to enhance and bring style to the interior of your house through the use of plants. Houseplants are similar to outdoor plants in that some give us a one-time show while others survive year after year, becoming a permanent accessory to their environment.

Houseplants A to Z will show you how to choose and care for your plants properly by providing a basic guide to growing and maintaining them, as well as specific information about individual varieties.

The presence of living plants in our surroundings gives us a feeling of tranquility, calmness, and relaxation, just as our outdoor gardens do. A happy houseplant will reward your efforts like those first new shoots in the springtime garden. You will learn to appreciate the cycles of houseplants once you live with and know them.

1. Good-quality potting soil specifically formulated for potted plants that is nutrient rich, light-to-medium weight, with a loose, fibrous texture and pleasant, musky scent. Some houseplants—azaleas, cacti, and orchids, for example—have special soil requirements, and it is best to purchase the ready-made mixes for these plants.

2. (see previous spread) Soil additives or substitutes, such as sand, shredded bark, perlite, and vermiculite, which will change the content and drainage of the soil mixture to better suit certain types of plants or containers.

3. Pure, fresh, clean water. See care tips 16–18.

4. A watering can with a long, narrow spout to reach the soil surface and disperse the water slowly and evenly.

5. Houseplant fertilizer. See care tip 74.

6a, 6b. A small fork and a trowel for potting, treating, and maintaining plants.

7. Clippers for trimming and grooming your plants. Clippers should be sharp to ensure a clean cut and have long, narrow blades for hard-to-reach places.

8. Pruning shears for trimming thick stems and branches.

9. Sharp knife for grooming and cutting away rotten roots and for dividing plants.

10. Gloves to protect hands from poisonous plants, disease, and pests. Medical or thin latex gloves are better than heavy gardening gloves, because they allow for more dexterity when planting and handling plants.

11. Coffee filters to keep soil and roots intact in newly potted containers.

12. Stakes of different sizes to support and train plants.

13. Twine and thread to secure plants to stakes in a variety of colors and thicknesses to suit different types of plants.

14. Various sizes of soft brushes and rags to use in cleaning and grooming your plants.

15. Mild soap, bleach, and rubbing alcohol for cleaning and grooming plants and to clean and sanitize tools, pots, and containers.

16. A mild pest and disease spray specifically for houseplants.

17. A magnifying glass to help identify hard-to-see pest and disease problems.

18. Misting bottles for fresh water to increase humidity and to apply fertilizer and insecticides topically. Be sure to use a mister that creates a fine vapor. See care tip 37.

19. Various types of pebbles or rocks for adding humidity to the plants and to improve drainage in certain containers. Make sure these rocks are washed and sanitized.

20. Moss to aid in water retention and to use in some potting methods.

21. Horticultural charcoal to help with freshness of soil and to aid in disease prevention.

22. A light and moisture meter to aid in proper watering and placement of plants.

23. Thermometer for accurate temperature readings.

24. Humidity gauge to indicate the level of moisture vapor in the air.

1

2

3

4

1. The size of the container should always be in proportion to the size of the plant. A pot that is too small will not hold enough soil to sustain the plant and its nutrient needs. A pot that is too large will house excess soil around the plant's roots, which may stay too wet and cause rot. Be aware that shallow pots can cramp and damage the root system of some plants, but they are useful for plants with shallow root systems.

2. Clay pots or containers made from porous materials will require more watering than other choices because water is readily absorbed through the material, causing the soil to dry out more rapidly. These pots are best for succulents and plants that like to dry slightly between waterings. Clay pots will create some humidity in the plant's environment as moisture is released through the porous material.

3. Plastic pots are inexpensive, lightweight, easy to handle, and unbreakable. They will keep soil moist longer than porous pots and are the best choice for moisture-loving plants.

4. Leave an inch or two between the soil level and the top of the pot or container. This will enable water to be absorbed into the soil and will keep the soil and water from spilling over the pot or container.

5. (no photo) Self-watering pots have a reservoir for water in their base. As the soil dries, it draws water from the reservoir. These pots are best for plants that prefer to be moist at all times.

Opposite: This ice-blue colored glass bowl complements the soft sage-green tones of the panda plant.

6. A terrarium is a clear glass container for displaying plants. Terrariums, which may be tightly closed or open, recycle their moisture and need very little attention. A closed terrarium can often go a month or more between waterings. Any clear container can be made into a terrarium; the main requirement is that it be watertight.

• Place a half-inch layer of small gravel in the bottom and sprinkle some horticultural charcoal on top.

• Put a thin layer of moss over the gravel-charcoal mixture to keep the soil layer intact.

• Fill to proper height with potting soil.

• Install plants, but leave room for growth. Push the soil aside, put a plant in the depression, and firm the soil around it.

• Water lightly, just a few ounces. Water lightly only after the plant gets dry once every few weeks. Do not fertilize. As the nutrients are used up, the plant's growth will slow down. Refresh the soil occasionally by scraping off the top layer and adding some fresh potting soil. This will add a small amount of needed nutrients.

• Place in a bright area, but not in direct sunlight. You should have enough light to read by. When the plant gets as big as you want, pinch off the newest growth to encourage bushier growth and to keep growth in control.

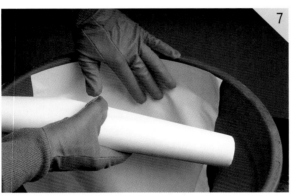

7. Porous containers can be made more watertight by lining the inside with heavy plastic or vinyl material. Cut the material to fit into the inside of the container and secure with a waterproof adhesive. Do not cover the drainage hole.

8. Good drainage is crucial to the health of your houseplants, and any container can work if drainage is monitored. Planting in a container without a drainage hole or a proper drainage reservoir can keep the soil too wet and cause roots to rot. Double-potting allows the use of containers without drainage holes. Simply place the existing pot or pots and plant as is into the larger, more decorative pot. Fill the space under and between the pots with moistened moss, soil, or stones. This creates a filtering layer to help disperse water. See care tips 23, 24, and 32.

9a, 9b. You may be tempted to transfer your new plant from the plain plastic pot to a more attractive container. Because switching pots can be stressful, you may run the risk of disturbing the plant's roots. Repotting is necessary only when roots meet their limit and need new room to grow. See care tips 80–83. Consider double-potting instead of disturbing your plant.

10. Pots should always be thoroughly washed and sanitized by adding a few drops of bleach to soapy water before use. Pests and disease can remain in pots and soil from previous plantings. A proper cleaning will ensure these do not spread to the new plant.

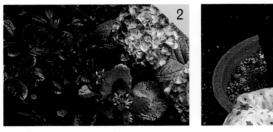

SELECTION AND LOCATION:

1. Always select the healthiest-looking houseplants. Be sure that the stems are strong and that there is even coverage of healthy leaves, with no yellow leaves or brown tips. The plants should be uniform in shape and not lopsided or uneven in growth. Avoid plants with dried soil or with roots growing out of the sides and bottom of the pot. Starting with healthy plants is the best way to be sure of success.

2. Flowering plants should have plenty of healthy, good-size buds. Avoid plants with tight green buds, which may not develop or open indoors. Flowering plants need to have most of the blossoms in the bud stage to ensure the longest display. A plant in full bloom will be more spectacular in the store, but the flowering time will be shorter.

3. Light, temperature, and humidity are all important factors in the location of houseplants and their survival. Know the origin of your plant—tropical, desert, and so on—and check the care tag for specific plant information, such as light, water, humidity, and feeding requirements. For best results, match the plant's requirements to its location in your home.

4. Plants grow under perfect conditions in nature and near-perfect conditions at the nursery or greenhouse. The conditions in your home are far less suitable, and plants may need a period of acclimatization to their new environment. Keep new plants out of direct sunlight and drafts and do not give them too much heat, water, or food. It is normal for the plant to drop a few leaves at first. After a couple of weeks of adjustment, most houseplants will grow just fine in the temperature and humidity levels of the average home.

5. (no photo) Moving a plant from one place to another to encourage growth can be a mistake. Be prepared for it to respond to the change, as it may drop its leaves or otherwise react poorly. Give the plant time to adjust to its new environment. Once you decide on a location, it is best to keep the plant in that spot. If the plant does not stabilize after a few weeks, it probably does need a new location—more or less light, warmer or cooler temperatures, extra humidity, and so on. It is important to pay attention to its needs and accommodate them.

6. Keep in mind that many houseplants are poisonous and should be carefully considered before purchasing, especially when children and pets are in the household. Many plants can cause serious reactions when handled, and illness and even death when ingested. Also, it is important to keep all plants out of reach of both children and pets, as handling or ingesting nonpoisonous varieties is never a good idea.

WATER:

7. Proper watering is essential for your plant's health and well-being. Besides the correct light exposure, water is the most important element in raising houseplants. Learn the watering needs of your plants and implement them accordingly. Most of us get into a routine of watering on a certain day or days, but each type of plant is different and watering needs differ as well. Proper watering should be practiced almost daily in the growing months of spring and summer and less often in fall and winter, which are the resting months.

8. Extremely cold water will shock even the toughest plant. Always use tepid water to water plants.

9. A basic method for determining when to water a plant is a touch test. If the soil looks dry and powdery, insert your finger into the top of the soil about one to two inches down. If the soil feels dry, the plant needs water. Other signs of dry soil are if the pot is light when you pick it up or makes a hollow sound when you tap on its sides.

10. A moisture meter is the best way to determine when to water your plants. Insert the meter at the top, middle, and bottom of the soil to get an accurate reading.

11. It is important to disperse the water slowly and evenly at soil level, being careful to not get too much water on the foliage. Also, be very careful not to drown the plant with a lot of water applied suddenly. This can shock the plant and disturb the soil and root system. The plant should be watered slowly until some water drains out of the bottom of the pot.

12. (opposite) Certain types of plants that need more water include:
   Fast-growing plants
   Plants that bear fruit and flowers
   Plants with a large total leaf surface, such as ferns (versus sparsely foliaged plants, such as palms or rubber plants)
   Plants with soft, lush foliage, such as ferns or ivies
   High-light plants that are exposed to a lot of bright, direct light (versus low-light plants in shaded locations)

13a

13b

Things that can affect how much water to give a plant are light exposure, moisture preference, container choice, growing conditions, and the soil mix.

13a. Water more when:
The container is porous, with clay or unglazed finishes.
The plant is actively growing, usually in the spring and summer.
The humidity level is lower.
The room temperature is warmer than normal.

13b. Water less when:
The container is plastic or has a glazed finish.
The plant is at rest, usually in the winter.
The humidity level is higher.
The room temperature is cooler than normal.

14. Succulents are a class of plants that usually originates in the desert and is characterized by thick, waxy, leathery, or swollen leaves and/or stems. These plants require much less water than other types of houseplants, since they have natural water-storing abilities in order to survive long periods of drought and heat in their natural environment. Water succulent plants in the growing season every two weeks to once a month, and in the resting winter months once a month to almost not at all. Always check the leaves; shriveling is a sign of thirst. See care tip 3.

15. (opposite) If a few of your plant's leaves are turning brown around the edges with dry, wilting leaves; if the lower leaves are curled or yellowing; or if flowers fall or quickly fade, then your plant needs more water.

If the entire plant wilts suddenly or if it has yellowing bottom leaves or soft and rotten areas at the base or moldy flowers or curled leaves, or brown mushy spots at the leaf base, or if both young and old leaves fall off at the same time, or if there is overall poor growth for no apparent reason, then your plant has been overwatered. See care tip 21.

14

16. Although tap water will suffice, it is not always right for watering plants because it may contain certain elements that can be harmful, such as fluoride and chlorine. See care tips 17 and 18. Rainwater is best but only in areas with little or no pollution; a better option is to purchase distilled water or use a water filter.

17. (no photo) Hard water can be harmful to your plants with its high concentration of minerals, but water-softening agents and devices can make the water high in sodium. See care tip 18.

18. (no photo) When watering plants with tap water, fill the bucket or watering can and let the water sit overnight. This will allow the minerals to settle to the bottom and bring the water to room temperature. It is a good idea to fill bottles or receptacles with water and store them near your plants. The water will be ready and at room temperature and always on hand when the plant needs water.

19. (no photo) Watering is best done in the morning because the warmer temperatures and brighter light during the day help with water absorption and the evaporation of any excess moisture on the foliage.

20. Watering plants from the bottom is a good method for plants with moisture-sensitive foliage, such as African violets and some succulents. Some plants, such as cyclamen, actually require bottom-watering to survive. Place the pot in an inch or two of water and allow the plants to slowly absorb moisture. Plants should take approximately twenty minutes to soak up sufficient water. Be careful to not leave these plants sitting in water for more time than is needed. See care tip 21.

21. (no photo) Over 90 percent of houseplant failure is caused by overwatering, which suffocates roots by depriving them of oxygen, which roots need in order to breathe and absorb water and nutrients. Some plants need a partial drying-out period before being watered, while others need constant moisture (but moist does not mean saturated). Know the individual water needs of your plants. See care tip 3.

22. Good drainage and proper watering practices go hand in hand. Never leave a plant sitting in water for too long. When you water your plants at the soil level, some of the water will drain into the receptacle or saucer underneath the pot. This water should always be emptied at once. A plant should sit in water no longer than twenty minutes, because the plant will continue to draw water into the soil and roots after having been properly watered, and this can be harmful. Stagnant water in receptacles or saucers can also become a host for pests and disease.

23. Double-potting is a good method for watering plants that like it on the dry side. See container tips 8 and 9. Add water to the moss or material between the pots. The water will be slowly absorbed into the interior pot.

24. Double-potting can also be accomplished with potting soil for plants that need to be watered from the bottom and that like to be relatively moist. Use the method described in care tip 23. Water the soil on which the plant is sitting. The water will be slowly absorbed by the plant without running the risk of taking up too much water. This is also a good way to feed plants because nutrients in the fresh soil will be absorbed with the water.

25. Most plants will recover from underwatering, but overwatering is usually fatal. Try letting the plant dry out before watering or repot it in fresh dry compost, and give the plant a few days before you resume a regular watering schedule. Also, trim off any unhealthy or rotten roots when repotting to help the plant heal. See care tip 83. If the plant does not improve in a few weeks, it may be best to discard it.

26. On occasion, moisture-loving plants or plants potted in a very porous potting medium, such as orchids, love to be soaked in a bucket or tub of water. Immerse the pot in warm water until the water just covers the rim of the pot. Use a fork to poke holes in the soil if the water is not being absorbed readily. Mist the foliage while the plant soaks. Soak plant about twenty minutes and allow it to drain thoroughly. Remove any excess water collected in the saucer.

27. (no photo) Soaking also works for plants that have been allowed to dry out completely and are stressed and wilted. If you notice your plant in this condition and the soil around the edges of the pot has shrunk from the sides, or if water runs completely through the pot without being absorbed by the plant, try care tip 26 to treat the plant. A plant that has wilted completely may survive, but you should expect to lose some leaves.

HUMIDITY:

28. (no photo) Plants thrive in relatively humid conditions, around 40 to 60 percent or more. Most homes have only 20 to 30 percent humidity, with even less in winter because of heating systems and in summer with air-conditioning. It is essential to supply extra humidity in order to maintain the health of houseplants. A humidifier is the best way to increase humidity for your house and your plants.

29. In general, plants with thin, delicate leaves, such as ferns and spider plants, need more humidity than plants with large, thick, waxy leaves, such as rubber plants, but every plant is different, so be familiar with the individual humidity needs of your plants. See care tip 3.

30. The main symptoms of low humidity are dry, brown leaf tips and curling leaves.

31. Plants continually release water vapor through openings in their leaves. This creates a moist layer of air, so grouping plants together will increase the overall humidity.

32. Another way to add humidity to a plant is to place a few clean pebbles or rocks at the base of the pot and add a little water, making sure that the water does not touch the soil or roots. The rock layer will also disperse whatever water drains from the pot and limit the plant's contact with water. See care tip 21.

33. Adding rocks to the inside base of your pot when planting will increase humidity.

34. You can also add extra humidity by keeping open receptacles of water, such as bowls or vases, near your plants.

35. Mulching a plant will keep the soil moist longer and increase humidity at the base and roots of the plant. See arranging tip 11.

36. Double-potting a plant also increases humidity. The material between the pots releases humidity when in contact with water. Remember to check this space periodically for water buildup. See container tips 8 and 9.

37. Frequent misting with a fine vapor of warm water is also a temporary fix for lack of humidity. Be sure to spray a few feet away from the plant, as extra water on the foliage and flowers of certain plants can be harmful. Keep in mind that you are adding humidity to the surrounding air, not to the actual plant. See care tip 38.

38. Too much moisture on the foliage can result in spotting and rot. Be sure to mist your plants in the morning, when conditions are more favorable for proper moisture absorption. See care tip 19. Never mist your plants in direct sun, as the water will reflect the light, magnify the rays, and burn the foliage. Never mist in a stagnant environment. See care tip 51.

39. Bathrooms and kitchens are usually more humid than other rooms, so put plants that require more or less constant humidity in these rooms. Be aware, however, that these rooms may also have more temperature fluctuations than other locations. See care tips 55–57 for proper temperature ranges.

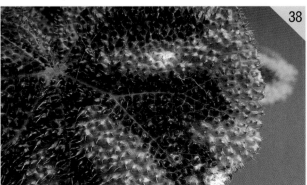

42

43

45

LIGHT:

40. (opposite) Plants need light for photosynthesis, which produces the food and energy necessary to keep them alive. Plants will not develop and grow properly without the correct light requirements, and the amount required will vary from one species to another. In general, however, most plants require eight to sixteen hours of light each day. See care tip 3.

41. (no photo). Match the right plant to the right light conditions for best performance. Plants are usually categorized as low-, medium-, or high-light plants:

- Low light: windows with partial eastern or northern exposure or the interior of a room.

- Medium light: windows with western or eastern exposure. Plants will also get medium light from partly shaded south-facing windows. Windows facing north give an even light without direct sun throughout the year.

- High light: directly in front of most south-facing windows or in large, unobstructed windows with western or eastern exposure. Windows facing south give direct sun in winter, but less in summer. Windows facing east and west give the most direct sun on a year-round basis.

42. The intensity of the light is as important as the length of daily exposure. Since the angle of the sun's rays changes throughout the year, many species grow best in one location during summertime and in a different spot during the winter. You may need to move your plants away from or closer to a window as the sun changes. South-facing windows see the greatest amount of seasonal change. More light enters a south window in winter than in summer, when the angle of the sun is lowest, although the intensity is less. Most plants in a sunny east or west window in the growing season may need to be moved to the southern location when the intensity drops in the fall and winter.

43. During the summer, bright, sunny windows may be too hot for most plants, and they may need to be placed a few feet away from the windows to prevent heat damage. These windows may be softened a bit by adding a blind or sheer curtain. Keep in mind that most plants thrive and bloom in bright filtered light conditions.

44. (no photo) The intensity of light drops off very rapidly as it enters the room, so a plant that is a few feet away from the window will get only half as much light as one close to the window. Always remember to place plants no more than six inches to one foot away from a direct light source for best performance.

45. If a plant performs poorly over time, it is important to move it into different light conditions. A yellow tinge, or white or brown spots, or patches on the leaves, or shriveled leaves may indicate that your plant is getting too much light. If your plant has become leggy and spindly, or leans to one side, or fails to grow at all, or looks weak and pale, it probably needs more light. Insufficient light may also cause the lower leaves to turn yellow or drop off.

46. (no photo) Because plants grow toward the light, turn your plants at least once a week to ensure that all sides get equal light exposure and maintain a nice, even shape.

47. Blooming and fruiting plants, as well as those with variegated leaves, require the brightest light indoors to perform to their full potential. Plants with solid, deep-green foliage tend to prefer medium to lower light. See care tips 3 and 41–45.

48. Reflected light will increase the amount of light in a room; light-colored walls, mirrors, skylights, and clean windows all help reflect light.

49. The best supplemental artificial light is a grow light, a special fluorescent light that provides almost the same spectrum as natural light. Regular fluorescent lights provide only partial needs for plants. Grow lights usually cost a little more, but they are very useful when there is not enough natural light available for plants.

50. (no photo) Plants characterized as low-light or shade plants cannot survive in areas with no light at all. They may do well without any direct light, but they eventually need a boost to survive. See arranging tips 5 and 6.

AIR CIRCULATION:

51. Proper air circulation is important for the health of your plants. Stagnant air can accumulate extra moisture on the plant and may promote pests and disease. A gentle, temperate, natural breeze is the best, but a ceiling fan or a room fan set on low will also help increase air circulation and the environment for your plants.

52. Plant roots also require air to maintain health. One way to improve air circulation to the roots of your plants is to create a space between the floor or saucer and the bottom of the pot by raising the container on some other support, such as a trivet, stones, or pot feet.

53. (no photo) Hot or cold air can damage plants, so avoid placing them near heat sources or air-conditioning vents. Most plants will react with a sudden leaf or bud drop.

54. Many plants benefit from a summer outdoors and being exposed to fresh air, natural sunlight, and rain, but acclimatize the plants slowly to the outside by keeping them in partial light and protected areas until they are accustomed to their new environment.

TEMPERATURE:

55. Most plants do best within a specific, constant temperature range, usually between 60° and 75°F. A slight fluctuation within this range is fine, but sudden changes can be damaging to most plants.

56. (no photo) Many plants like a change of temperature in different seasons, usually a warmer location during their active growth and a slightly cooler one while they rest in winter. They also like the temperature to be five to ten degrees cooler at night. These temperature ranges and changes resemble the natural environment. Evening temperatures about ten degrees cooler can trigger blooms in orchids and many other flowering plants.

57. (no photo) To give plants a constant temperature in winter, when the sun is lower in the sky and the intensity of light is weaker, move them from a cool northern window to an eastern or western location, and move plants from an eastern or western location to a southern location. This move will give the plants a more consistent year-round environment with regard to both temperature and light. See care tip 42.

58. Plants need protection from cold, wind, and heat to prevent damage, so be sure to protect them on the trip home from the nursery or store with proper wrapping.

60a,b

61

62

SOIL:

59. (opposite) The right soil mixture is essential for the health and life of your plants. The primary purpose of soil is to support or anchor the plant in its container, to slowly release small amounts of nutrients, and to retain moisture and allow for good drainage. Several plants need special mixtures or additives to be happy and healthy. Knowing the soil type and mixture for each of your plants and accommodating their needs will benefit your plants in the long run. See basic tools 1 and 2.

There are two types of potting soil mixtures:

60a. Soil-less: Some potting soils are not soil at all but a combination of sterile inorganic and organic materials (at left in photo above). Most mixes are lightweight and contain such ingredients as perlite, vermiculite, sand, and peat moss. These mixes have excellent drainage and water-absorbing qualities and are handy for large containers, but they need to be fertilized more frequently, owing to the lack of natural nutrient content. Keep in mind that mixes containing perlite also contain fluoride, which is harmful to some plants.

60b. Soil-based: Potting soil that contains organic matter is slightly heavier and darker than the soil-less mixtures. Because soil-based potting soil has its own mineral content and releases a constant, small stream of nutrients to the plant roots, you will need less supplemental fertilizer.

61. Good soil should be light but substantial to the touch; the soil should be easily sifted through. If the soil feels claylike or heavy, it will probably suffocate the plant and its roots. Make sure your soil does not have large chunks of wood or debris. These are unnecessary fillers and are not what your plants need.

62. Heavier soil, usually sold in bags marked as garden soil or topsoil, is useful for planting and anchoring larger plants. The slightly sturdier mix will pack around the base of the plant and roots to stabilize the plant for proper growth.

63. (no photo) The more nutrient-rich and sterile the soil, the better for the health of the plant, so always use a good-quality, sanitized potting mixture rather than soil directly from your garden. Garden soil may contain disease and pests that can flourish in the warm, confined environment of a home or interior setting.

64. (no photo) Do not reuse soil from one plant or pot for another plant. The nutrients are most likely depleted and may contain disease and pests from other plants or pots. Always buy new bags of soil for your plants.

65. Soil additives such as sand, gravel, and bark are useful for improving the content of the soil mixture by increasing its drainage and moisture-retentive qualities. Although most plants are happy in a standard soil mixture, some, including bulbs and orchids, need more specialized environments. Be sure to use sterile additives; it is best if they are labeled for specific plant use, such as "orchid bark."

66. Most plants will benefit if their pots are given a good scrubbing and some fresh soil. This is commonly referred to as "freshening the pot." Gently remove the plant from its original container without interrupting the root system and put it in a temporary container. See care tips 83a and 83b. Thoroughly scrub the pot with a bleach-and-soap mixture and rinse thoroughly. Add a thin layer of fresh potting soil to the bottom of the pot. Gently replace the plant into the original container, and top with a thin layer of fresh potting soil. See container tips 2 and 10.

67. Soil polymers are gels that absorb hundreds of times their weight in water and release it as the soil dries. Mixed into potting soil, gels keep both water and nutrients available near plant roots and enable you to extend the time between waterings. Polymers are most useful in dry climates, in soil mixes for moisture-loving plants, and in containers that tend to dry out quickly. Some soil mixes come with polymers already incorporated, but you can easily mix them into your soil mix when repotting. Stick to the manufacturer's recommendations, and remember: Soil that stays too wet can kill your plants. See care tip 21.

68. When planting or potting with fresh potting soil, it is important to mix some water into the soil before putting it into the container. Potting soil is lightweight and will float to the top of the container, making a mess when watered. In a separate container, mix the soil with water just until the soil can be held together when you grab a fistful. Make sure the soil holds together but that excess water does not drain out when squeezed. This indicates the soil is too wet, and you should add more dry soil to the mix.

FOOD:

69. (no photo) Proper nutrients are essential for a plant's health, and plants must be fed regularly according to individual needs. A general houseplant fertilizer is acceptable for all of your houseplants, but it is best to have a specific one for foliage plants and one for flowering plants. A more specialized fertilizer may be necessary for certain types of plants, such as orchids and African violets. See care tip 3.

70. The three numbers on the fertilizer package indicate the proportions by weight of the three basic nutrients contained in the food: nitrogen, phosphorus, and potassium, all necessary for healthy plant growth. The first number refers to nitrogen, essential for leaf growth and rich, green foliage; the second number is for phosphorus, which promotes healthy root development and flower and fruit production. The last number is potassium, essential for overall plant development, health, and disease resistance. In general fertilizer the three numbers are equal or nearly so; for flowering plants, select one with a higher middle number. Good fertilizers usually add secondary nutrients, such as copper, iron, magnesium, zinc, and calcium.

71. (no photo) Most plants are fed only when they are growing actively and when the light and temperature are such that they can take advantage of additional nutrients. Feed plants during the summer, giving them less food in spring and autumn, and none in winter. Watch for signs of slowing activity late in the season; and cut back on watering and fertilizing. This adaptation to seasonal changes is natural and necessary. It can be detrimental to a plant's health to force growth with fertilizer and light during resting periods.

72. Winter-flowering plants, such as cyclamen, azaleas, orchids, or plants growing under artificial lights, are an exception to the general rule noted above.

73. (no photo) A new plant from a greenhouse does not need to be fertilized right away, as it has probably been given the sufficient amount. Wait a month or two before feeding.

74a. Plant fertilizer generally comes in several forms: liquid, pellets, sticks, pills, and granules. Liquid fertilizers are the quickest-acting and are best to use when the plant needs an immediate boost. Liquid fertilizers can be diluted and used at each watering or used at full strength sparingly, usually once or twice a month. It is best to use the diluted method at each watering for flowering plants.

74c

74d

79

74b. (opposite) Powders or granular forms are dissolved into water and can be used as a liquid formula, as in care tip 74a, or sprinkled on the top of the soil. Use a small garden rake or fork to scratch the food into the soil surface.

74c. Slow-release fertilizers are most useful when added directly to the soil. It is good to do this when repotting a plant. The bead form can be mixed into the compost. The sachet form can be placed at the bottom of the pot. Keep in mind that slow-release fertilizers respond to temperature and light and will not stop releasing nutrients in winter as they would for an outside plant. Be careful, therefore, not to use these fertilizers later in the season.

74d. Sticks and pellets are easy and can just be pushed into the soil. This method is least desirable, however, as the fertilizer may release nutrients unevenly, creating hot spots or heavy concentrations of fertilizer in the soil, which can damage the roots and plant.

75. (no photo) Never fertilize a plant that has dry soil. Make sure the soil is moist before applying fertilizer.

76. (no photo) Remember that low-light plants need less fertilizer than high-light ones.

77. (no photo) Keep in mind that plants grow slower indoors and that if a general fertilizer is used, it should be at approximately one-quarter the recommended strength.

78. (no photo) Do not overfeed! More is not always better. Always read the manufacturer's instructions for the recommended amount, and note that these recommendations are usually for liquid fertilizers only and do not apply to time-release options. Overfertilizing can produce burning of the tips and roots and kill your plants.

79. Flushing a plant to remove the buildup of fertilizer is an essential chore. Fertilizer salts can accumulate in a container and in the soil, a condition indicated by a hard, white powdery film on the soil surface or the inside edges of the container. Simply run water through the soil several times to flush away the salts and then drain properly. Try to do this every one or two months. Limit the buildup of salts by using horticultural charcoal when repotting. See care tips 66 and 83h.

REPOTTING AND DIVISION:

80. (no photo) Repotting and division will rejuvenate the plant and allow it more room to grow. This is best done at the beginning of or during the growing season—spring and early summer. It is not wise to repot or divide in the resting months of winter.

81. Repotting and division are necessary when a plant's roots fill the space inside the pot and the plant needs more room to keep growing. Signs of a pot-bound or root-bound plant are: the lower leaves turn yellow, the plant needs constant watering, the roots are growing out of the container or the drainage hole in the bottom of the pot, or a plant is hard to remove from the pot and resists when you try to remove it.

82. When you remove the plant and find a mass of tangled white roots, it is time for repotting. If only a few white roots are visible, your plant is fine and does not need this process. Place your plant back in the pot and continue care.

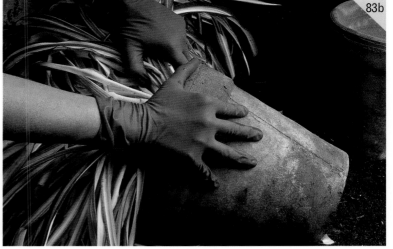

STEPS FOR REPOTTING:

83a. A few hours before repotting, thoroughly water the plant before removing it from the pot. If the plant tugs back when you try to remove it, loosen the plant by running a knife or spatula around the edges or tapping it a few times on a hard surface.

83b. Gently remove the plant from the existing pot.

83c. Support the plant when removing it from the pot by cradling it in your hand or laying it on its side. Try not to damage the foliage or flowers during this process. It is a good idea to support the plant by propping it up a few inches to prevent damage to the foliage and flowers.

83d. Gently pull away some of the tangled roots to free them from the mass, so they will be able to root and grow into the new soil. Clip away any rotten or damaged roots.

83e. If you wish to return the plant to the same pot or to a new pot of the same size, or keep the plant the same size, then trim away about one inch of the root-ball all the way around. Remember, you must also trim away some of the foliage to make up for the fewer roots, or you will lose several leaves when the plant reestablishes itself. Never trim off more than one-third of the root-ball to maintain health, and always trim the long roots that spiral under the root-ball.

83f. (no photo) If you want a plant to grow bigger, use a pot only an inch or two bigger than the old pot. This will provide plenty of room for the plant to thrive. A pot that is too large may harm the plant by holding too much moisture (see container tip 21), or it may allow the roots to grow too much and not reserve enough energy for top growth.

83g. Place a coffee filter in the bottom of the pot over the drainage hole. This will help keep the new soil intact until the roots are established and will allow the water to drain properly. Put a layer of new soil in the bottom of the container. See care tip 68. (Adding a slow time-release fertilizer to the new potting soil is okay, but it is not a good idea to regularly fertilize a newly repotted plant for at least one month. The roots need time to recover from the stress of repotting before they are encouraged to grow with fertilizer.)

83h. Add a sprinkling of horticultural charcoal to the bottom mixture to keep the soil fresh and aid in proper nutrient absorption. See basic tools 21.

83i. Center the plant and fill in with moistened soil, firming it gently around the edges and the root-ball. See container tip 3. Water the plant evenly and thoroughly and put it in a shady spot for a few days to give the plant time to establish itself.

Division is another method for rejuvenating a plant that has overgrown its setting. Dividing helps maintain a plant's size and shape and will also provide you with one or more additional plants; it is also the method used for separating offsets or "pups" from a mature plant. See care tip 88. For plants with fibrous root systems:

84a. Water the plant a few hours before division, so the plant can easily be removed from the pot.

84b. Remove the plant from the pot and put it on its side, doing your best to protect the foliage and flowers.

84c. Pull or cut the root-ball in half, making sure each section has a cluster of leaves and plenty of roots. You can divide your plant into three or more parts, if there are plenty of roots to support the leaves and to reestablish the plant in its new setting.

84d. Repot each half or section into individual pots that are the appropriate size for the new plant. See care tips 83g–83i.

85. Plants with multiple crowns, usually apparent by several clusters of growing tips of the plant, may be divided by separating the sections of crowns into individual plants with the roots attached. Repot the same as above.

PROPAGATION AND STARTING NEW PLANTS:

86. (opposite) Many plants can be started from leaf or stem cuttings of the original plant. Simply cut a mature leaf, allow the end to dry for a few minutes, and place it stem down in a pot of fresh soil with the leaf resting on top of the soil. See care tip 68. Within a few weeks, roots will develop and a new plant will eventually emerge from the base of the original leaf. Placing a clear plastic bag over the pot will create a greenhouse effect and may help speed things along.

87. Many plants can also be started by rooting stems or leaves in water. Cut a section of stem or a mature leaf, and place it in warm water. Put the glass with the cutting in good light, preferably next to a window. In several days roots will appear. When the roots are well established, the cutting can be planted in new soil. See care tip 68.

88. Some plants will produce smaller plants called pups or offsets. These small plantlets are at the base of the main plant or mother plant. Let the plantlets get approximately one-third the size of the mother plant before dividing. Make sure the plantlets have sufficient roots to establish when repotted in their own container. See care tip 84.

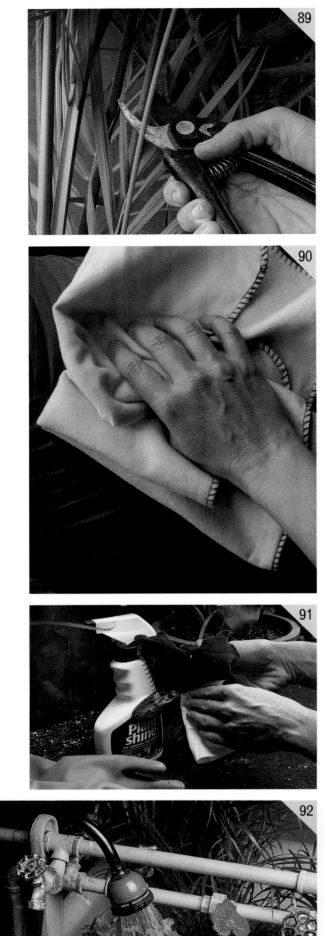

PRUNING AND GROOMING:

89. Pruning and grooming are necessary to maintain the appearance, shape, and size of your plants and will also help promote new growth. It is important to groom a plant at least once a month, if not more often. This is the time to clean and inspect the plant carefully. Dust and dirt can clog the pores of plants and inhibit the absorption of light and water and the process of photosynthesis, through which plants produce energy for growth.

90. When dusting leaves, always use a dry brush or a dry cloth. Use water only if the plant is greasy or extremely dirty. If the leaves appear to have a lot of buildup, you may use a mild soap solution. Mix a few drops of mild soap into a bucket of warm water and wipe and clean the leaves gently.

91. Leaf wipes or a leaf-shine product will also work, but use these very sparingly, as they contain wax and other substances likely to build up on the leaves. This buildup can block the pores of the leaves and prevent light and air from penetrating the leaves for growth and health.

92. Many plants can benefit from a dowsing or tepid shower. This is also a good way to groom plants with very small leaves and to remove dust and buildup on larger-leaved plants. See care tip 8. It is important to cover the pot and soil with plastic wrap or aluminum foil to prevent the soil from moving and the plant from getting overwatered. Dip the foliage in a deep bucket or tub of water several times or place in the shower for several minutes. Allow the plant to dry properly. See care tip 19.

93. Fuzzy or hairy-leafed plants or cacti should be groomed with a small soft brush, since excess moisture can be damaging to this type of foliage and plant.

94. (no photo) Pruning should make the plant look better by keeping it a certain size or achieving a certain shape. Not all plants need pruning, but many will benefit from the practice, which encourages growth and can correct structural problems or damaged growth caused by disease and pests. It is important to know your plant before you begin to prune, so that you know what to cut off and what to not cut off. Many plants are slow growers, and if you remove too much of a plant or a major branch, it will take a long time to grow back.

95. To encourage a bushy and more uniform plant, cut or pinch back any new weak growth. This will encourage the plant to concentrate its energy on producing healthy, full growth.

96. Always remove yellow or brown leaves from a plant, as well as spotted or wilted leaves. If you leave dead or dying leaves on a plant, you may encourage the growth of molds and other diseases. Do not use scissors to trim the spots or parts of leaves that are turning yellow or browning. The leaves will continue to turn at the cut edges and will seem repaired only temporarily.

97. Removing dead blossoms from a flowering plant (deadheading) not only improves its appearance but also encourages new blossoms to open and develop properly.

98. When staking plants, use stakes only as a temporary fix. If a plant needs a permanent stake to survive, there is something wrong and it is best to drastically trim the plant or throw it away.

99. (no photo) Stakes can be permanent for climbing plants or plants that are being permanently trained into a standard or form or as a decorative addition. See arranging tip 16.

100. When staking a plant, be sure not to damage the stem. Tie a tight knot to the stake, a loose figure eight around the plant stem, and another knot to the stake. This will allow the stem to be trained but will not cause damage as the plant grows. Support a plant in a few spots, not just one. This reduces the chances of major breakage.

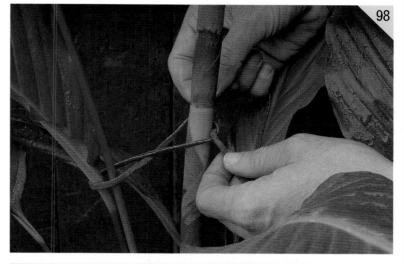

101

102

PROBLEMS:

101. Vigorous plants are the best defense against disease and pests. The more robust and healthy your plant, the greater the resistance. Properly caring for and maintaining your plants are the best form of prevention. Poor light, over- or underwatering, over- or underfertilizing, the wrong temperature and humidity, unsuitable potting mix, and pests can all cause problems and disease.

102. Diseased or weakened plants are usually indicated by yellow or spotted leaves, molds and mildews, stickiness on the leaves and stems, and stunted growth or leaf drop.

103. Always cut off and destroy diseased portions of any plant to avoid spreading disease to other parts of the plant and to other healthy plants. Wash and sanitize your tools with rubbing alcohol after use.

104. (no photo) The best way to identify pests on your plants is by the damage they do, so take note of any abnormality. See care tip 102. Since infestations can go unnoticed at an early stage, owing to the small size of the pests, use a magnifying glass to help determine if there are pests on your plants. See basic tools 17.

105. Always check the underside of a plant's foliage before and after you purchase it, as this is where pests are usually present. A proper initial inspection and regular checking will help prevent pests from infesting your plants.

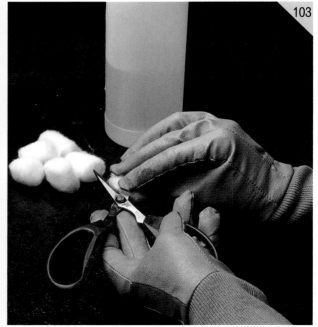

103

105

106. Once you notice signs of pests or disease, isolate the infested plant from other plants and treat it until the problem is cleared up, which may take three weeks to a month or more. Wash diseased plants by hand or under running water from a hose or faucet, and be sure to get the undersides of leaves as well. Use tepid water and a little mild soap to clean your plant. See care tip 90. Spray your plant with a mild pest and disease spray. Also, dunking the foliage upside down in a tub of water to which a few drops of insecticidal soap has been added is another way to treat your plant. See care tip 92. Repeat this process every week if necessary. Plants can also be treated by wiping the infected areas with rubbing alcohol on a cotton ball or cloth. During treatment, move plants to a cooler location and out of direct sunlight until the problem is under control.

107. Highly refined oils sold as horticultural oils are also very effective in controlling some pests. The oil suffocates the insects when applied. Always follow label directions to avoid damage to some plants that may be sensitive. Horticultural oils are nontoxic and safe to use, but be careful to protect surfaces from residue during treatment.

108. When the pests are visible to the eye, it usually means that too much damage has been done and it is too late to save the plant. Catching problems quickly and beginning immediate treatment may work, but once a plant has taken a turn for the worse from disease or pests, it is best to discard it. Pests and disease can easily spread to other healthy plants.

109. (no photo) Treatments are different for specific problems, and it is important to identify them before beginning treatment. It is a good idea to take an infected leaf sample to a nursery to find out the exact problem and treatment.

110a

110b

110c

110d

The most common plant pests are as follows:

110a. Aphids, sometimes called plant lice, are the most common houseplant pest. These tiny, round-to-pear-shaped insects secrete a sticky dew when sucking out the plant juices and are particularly fond of new growth shoots on plants. These pests may be white, brown, black, green, or red. See care tip 106.

110b. Mealy bugs are tiny, soft, white insects that cluster at the base of leaves or stems, where they resemble puffs of cotton. Mealy bugs suck the sap from the plant and also leave sticky dew on the leaves. Remove with cotton balls and rubbing alcohol. See care tip 106.

110c. Scale insects look like little bumps on stems or on the undersides of leaves. They are usually yellow or pale brown and leave traces of sticky dew on the plant leaves, which will yellow and wilt and may drop off. Scale insects must be scraped off, since their protective shell shields them from sprays and oils. Follow up by wiping leaves with rubbing alcohol. See care tip 106.

110d. Spider mites can be identified by the small spider webs they make, often mistaken for dust. Yellow dots will appear on the leaves as the spider mites suck out the plant juices. The plant will have an overall dull appearance. See care tip 106.

110e. (no photo) White flies are small white moths that rest on the undersides of leaves and fly off when the foliage is disturbed. These tiny insects are usually only visible in motion. White flies also excrete sticky dew and can cause spotting and yellowing of leaves. See care tip 106.

VACATION TIME:

111a, 111b. It is a real problem to keep plants alive when you are away, unless you have a reliable friend to watch over things. If you are away for just a few days, it may be helpful to group your plants together, since this will create a more humid environment. See care tip 31. If you are away for longer, group all of your plants together in your bathtub with a little water, just enough to lightly water your plants without damaging them. See care tip 21. Place a few bricks in the tub to support plants that do not need the extra water. The porous material will absorb the water and create extra humidity for all of the plants without over-watering.

112. For longer trips, water your plants thoroughly and place them in individual, lightly sealed, clear plastic bags. Put them in medium to low light, never direct light. The moisture created inside the bag will help keep your plants alive for a week or maybe more. Be sure to check for bugs and disease before enclosing the plant in this moist environment, and slowly acclimatize it to its normal routine of light and water after you return.

1. (opposite) Plants are great accent pieces and decorating tools for adding color, texture, and style to your home. You may select a plant primarily to match your decor or to create a striking focal point. A living or growing element added to a room can create a mood, fill a space, or complete a setting.

2. Look for plants that fit your style and complement your home. White orchids or a graceful palm can add an exotic flair to a contemporary setting, while showy hydrangeas and lush ivies enhance a romantic Victorian style or traditional home.

3. (no photo) Houseplants can be changed or moved, which makes them the perfect design element since they are not a permanent fixture. Plants are also an inexpensive way to alter your interior.

4. Plants can be a long-term decorative choice for the right space in a particular room that may also have the right conditions for a plant to thrive year after year. A large ficus tree or an interior window box of cascading ivy can be a handsome permanent feature.

5. Some plants that require a lot of light, such as spectacular flowering plants like the kalanchoe below, may look good in areas of your home with low light conditions, such as the dining-room table. These plants can be used in such areas as long as they are periodically rotated to a sunny spot. Place the plant in the ideal location for about a week, and then move it to a well-lighted location to recover and flourish. It is advisable to purchase two plants of the same type to alternate between the two locations.

6

8

10

6. Plants can be used like cut flowers to accent a room or home. Some plants used for decorative purposes may not be kept in the best location for their long-term well-being, but they will usually last much longer than cut flowers.

7. (opposite) Many outdoor flowering and green plants can be used inside temporarily as accent pieces for decorative purposes. Sometimes the outdoor plants at your nursery or greenhouse are the showiest and most interesting. These sleek pots of black mondo grass are a striking centerpiece for this living-room table. A pot of lavender can be a perfect bathroom accent; sunny sunflower plants are great in a kitchen window. Seasonal plants at holidays, such as daisies at Easter or juniper plants at Christmas, can provide attractive decorative accents.

8. Houseplants are also useful for covering up the problem areas or filling in bare or unused spaces in a room. If you like your window but not the view, a plant is the perfect solution. Empty areas, such as an unused fireplace or a bare corner, are wonderful filled temporarily with plants.

9. (no photo) Choose a plant close to the size you want for the particular space you intend to fill. Houseplants can be slow growers, and you may have to wait a while to get the look you want if you choose a small specimen.

10. Containers are a great way to accent a particular plant and create a finishing touch to a room or a space. A container can change the appearance of a plant and make almost any variety work in a setting.

11. Attractive mulch will enhance the look of a plant as it serves the useful purpose of holding moisture in the soil. Stones, moss of all types, and sand can all be used to top-dress a plant. Ground-cover plants, such as moss, ivy, and baby tears, can also serve as mulch and add a natural look to the plant. The ground covers should share the same requirements as the main plant. See care tip 3.

12. (opposite) Mixing plants together to form arrangements is a great way to combine different textures and colors and to create larger displays. Remember to make sure that all the plants have similar water and light needs.

13. Although houseplants can be planted together in a single pot, it is better to group individual plants in separate pots in a larger container. This way the root systems will not be disturbed, and you will be able to use more varieties of plants together and rearrange them more easily.

14. When combining and arranging different potted plants, choose a waterproof container or one with a drainage receptacle to ensure that excess water from the various plants will either be contained or have a proper place to drain.

15. If the container is deeper than some or all of the plants being used, you can use extra terra-cotta pots, bricks, stones, or any sturdy materials to build up certain plants to the level of the container opening. Leave enough room between the plants to water and groom them properly.

17

18

19

16. (opposite) Stakes are used to support and train certain plants but can also be used to accent a plant and its presentation. The best stakes are made from natural materials, such as branches from trees and shrubs or bamboo. Choose a stake that will blend in with the plant as attractively as possible. See care tips 98–100.

17. Foliage from many houseplants makes a great accent for cut-flower arrangements or on its own. You can even use the attractive leaves of unhealthy plants or plants on their way out. Cut foliage has a long vase life and can be reused several times with cut flowers. Before discarding a plant, cut the healthy leaves and arrange them in a vase alone or with a few flowers. Smoky rex begonia leaves make a striking backdrop for these bright flowers. See care tip 87.

18. In addition to being decorative accents, plants also reduce indoor pollution and provide for a healthier environment. Plants release oxygen and absorb our carbon dioxide, but they also absorb air pollutants and toxic chemicals through their leaves. Growing several houseplants can significantly reduce pollutants in an average home or workplace.

19. Many plants, both green and flowering, make wonderful holiday decorations.

HOUSEPLANTS A to Z

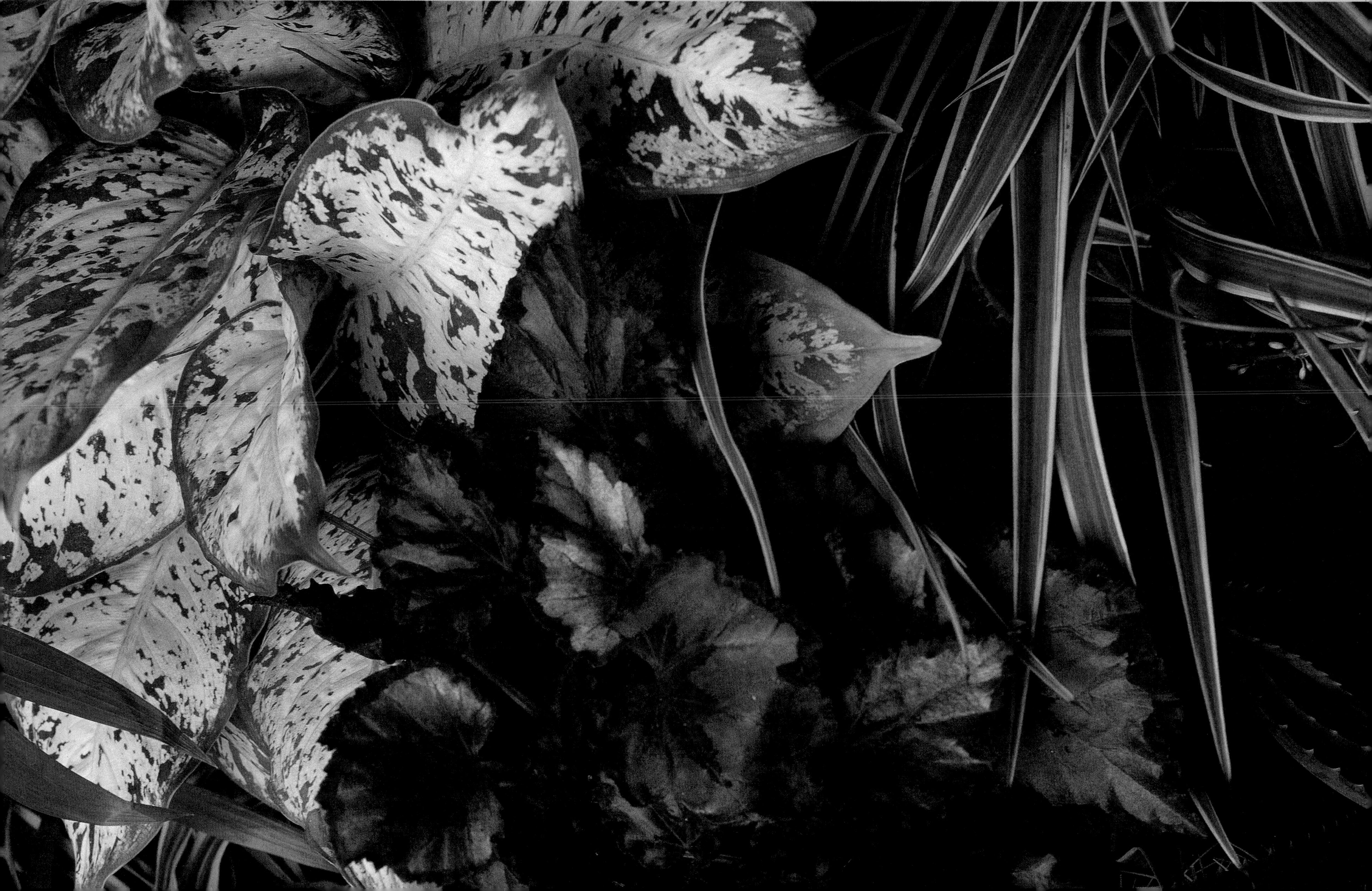

NAME: African violet, saintpaulia.
VARIETIES: There are more than 20,000 saintpaulia varieties in many colors and combinations.
SEASON: Available all year.
COLOR: Pinks, magenta, white, blue, purples, lavender, a rare red, bicolors with contrasting edging or throat colors, even a striped variety.
SCENT: None.
LIGHT: Bright light, but not direct sun. See care tip 41. These plants like twelve to sixteen hours of light a day and require eight hours of complete darkness.
TEMPERATURE: Between 65° and 72°F. Will not perform well above 80° or below 60°F. Avoid sudden temperature changes or drafts.
WATER: Slightly moist at all times. It is best to water these plants from the bottom. See care tips 8, 16–22, and 24.
HUMIDITY: High. Do not mist, as water can spot the leaves and flowers. See care tips 32–36 and 38.
FOOD: Feed at each watering during flowering time with diluted solution of African violet food or a fertilizer that promotes flower production. See care tip 70. Plants will benefit from a twice-a-month feeding even when not in flower, since they can bloom any time of the year.
SOIL: Soil specially made for these plants is the correct density and is enriched with some essential nutrients. The roots are very small and require a light, rich soil that drains well. Do not pack the soil down. African violets should not be repotted often but only when the plant starts to grow up, the base stem is exposed, and the leaves do not rest against the sides of the pot. Being slightly root-bound may encourage flower production. See care tip 83.
PROPAGATION: Leaf cuttings. See care tip 86.
PESTS AND PROBLEMS: Aphids, white flies, and mealy bugs. See care tip 110. Excess moisture on the flowers and foliage can result in mold.
TIP: Sometimes a plant will have healthy growing leaves but no flowers from lack of sufficient light. Move your plant to a brighter location. Remove the larger side shoots of leaves to channel energy into producing flowers. Keep free of dust. See care tips 93 and 97.
NOTE: African violets are popular as desk plants, because they can grow and thrive in the normal, cool-white, fluorescent lighting conditions found in many offices and buildings.

1. African violets are small flowering plants with violetlike flowers held upright in clusters above the rosette of soft leaves. Healthy plants will bloom for about three months or more and then rest.

2. Most common African violets have plain, dark green leaves with single purple flowers, but novelty varieties have double flowers, ruffled leaves, two-tone colors, variegated leaves, and more. Plants with solid green leaves and purple flowers are much hardier and easier to grow than the novelty types.

3. The common, deep-purple varieties are striking when massed together to form a spring meadow centerpiece. Use any watertight decorative container and double-pot the plants. See container tip 8 and arranging tips 13–15.

4. A single novelty variety in a simple pot adds a delicate touch to any desk or windowsill.

NAME: Aloe, aloe vera, burn plant.

VARIETIES: About 300 species of aloe exist, ranging from the tallest "tree aloe," which can reach sixty feet, to the smallest plant of just a few inches. The most common houseplant variety is the aloe vera (Aloe barbadensis).

SEASON: Available all year.

COLOR: Pale, grayish-green leaves with hints of speckles or spotted margins. Orange, yellow, red, or cream-colored lilylike flowers grow atop a spikelike stem that may appear in summer.

SCENT: None.

LIGHT: High-light plant. See care tip 41. Will tolerate lower light conditions for extended periods.

TEMPERATURE: Between 55° and 70°F. Aloes will not tolerate cold.

WATER: Aloes are succulents. See care tip 14.

HUMIDITY: Average to low.

FOOD: Fertilize once each year during the spring or summer.

SOIL: Aloes like sandy, well-drained soil, so a mix of 50 percent sand and 50 percent loose soil is ideal. Cactus mixes are also excellent. Because of its slow growth habit, an aloe may stay in its pot for many months to years. The root system spreads outward, so choose a pot that is wide rather than deep when repotting. Drainage is very important for aloe care. See care tip 22.

PROPAGATION: Aloes are propagated by offsets and make a wonderful gift. See care tip 88.

PESTS AND PROBLEMS: Rare.

TIP: Aloe is the ideal low-maintenance houseplant. It does not have to be groomed or pruned; you can forget to water it and fail to give it proper light, and it will wait patiently for you. The only conditions this hardy plant cannot tolerate are over-watering and cold temperatures.

MEANING: The aloe is believed to attract luck, guard against negative influences, and help prevent household accidents.

NOTE: The aloe contains many active compounds, including vitamins, minerals, enzymes, proteins, and amino acids. Aloe vera gel is used as a base for nutritional drinks, healing products, and cosmetics for skin and hair care, among other products. Cleopatra is said to have attributed her beauty to aloe and massaged fresh aloe gel into her skin to make it glow.

1. Aloes form lush rosettes with their thick, tapered leaves and range from a few inches to three feet in length. Many aloes, if grown under the proper conditions, bear pretty spikes of tubular flowers in summer.

2. No kitchen is complete without a spiky aloe plant in a sunny nook, ready and waiting to soothe minor burns, cuts, bug bites, rashes, and sunburns. Cut off a leaf and peel back a portion of its skin before applying. Aloe sap is a thick gel and dries quickly.

3. Tiger or partridge breast aloe (Aloe variegata) is a dwarf variety with rosettes of dark green leaves with white crossbands and small red-tipped white teeth on the edges.

4. The hardy aloe plant is an ideal choice to add great architectural lines and texture to an interior setting. See arranging tips 5 and 6.

NAME: Azalea, rhododendron.

VARIETIES: The most common houseplant azalea is Rhododendron simsii, and it is available in single and double varieties, as well as some novelty ones.

SEASON: Winter to spring.

COLOR: Red, pinks, magenta, white, peach, bicolors with contrasting edging or throat colors.

SCENT: Some have a slightly sweet fragrance.

LIGHT: Bright light, but no direct sun. See care tip 41.

TEMPERATURE: Likes to be on the cooler side, around 50° to 60°F. If your plant flowers only for a short time or if the flowers suddenly drop or if your plant dies prematurely, the temperature is probably too warm.

WATER: Water often but avoid complete sogginess. See care tips 21, 22, and 24. A plant that drops buds and leaves after about a week has been allowed to dry out and will benefit from a good soak. Azaleas have dense root-balls, and the soak will ensure that all the roots get adequate moisture. See care tip 26; also important are care tips 16–19.

HUMIDITY: High. See care tips 31–37. Leaves will shrivel from lack of moisture.

FOOD: Not necessary if you buy your plant in flower. See "Care after Flowering" below.

SOIL: Newly purchased azaleas can benefit from "freshening the pot" with a heavier soil mixture; see care tip 66. Azaleas are sold planted in a very light, peat-enriched soil that does not easily retain moisture. Azaleas do not tolerate lime, so use a soil mixture that is lime-free. Many stores carry a mixture especially made for azaleas and rhododendrons.

PESTS AND PROBLEMS: Spider mites. See care tip 110.

TIP: Because azaleas tend to dry out and need constant moisture and humidity, it is best to double-pot them. See container tip 8 and care tips 24 and 36.

NOTE: Poisonous. See care tip 6.

CARE AFTER FLOWERING: Azaleas can be brought into flower again, but the process is lengthy and may not be worth the effort. To try, carefully remove the dead flowers at the base above the cluster of leaves, but do not damage new growth buds. Move the plant to a cool room (50°F) and water as usual. Repot using a lime-free potting mix. See care tip 83. Place the pot in the ground in a partially shady spot in the garden and continue to water and feed twice a month until early autumn or before danger of frost. Dig up the pot and take it into a cool room. Cut back on the watering and wait for buds to appear. Move to lighter and slightly warmer conditions when the plant is in bud and resume a regular watering schedule. Beautiful!

1. The azalea belongs to a large family of evergreen shrubs, most familiar as garden plants. This dwarf variety, Rhododendron simsii, is widely sold as a houseplant and reaches twelve to sixteen inches in height, with round leathery leaves and bell-shaped flowers.

2. Purchase azaleas with a few flowers open and with masses of large buds and healthy, deep-green leaves with no yellowing.

3. Azaleas are one of the best ways to have big, showy flowers growing indoors during the gloomy winter and early spring months. Since azaleas crave bright light and cooler temperatures, they are a good choice for an interior window box. These azaleas thrive in the window of this cool bedroom.

NAME: Baby tears, angel tears, helxine.

VARIETIES: The most common for houseplant use are Helxine soleirolii and Soleirolia soleirolii varieties.

SEASON: Available all year.

COLOR: Bright green to silvery green.

SCENT: None.

LIGHT: Bright, filtered light is best. Plants can survive in lower light conditions but may become pale and leggy. The small leaves begin to droop, and the vinelike stems become tangled and discolored. Give these plants sufficient light to retain their healthy clump appearance and trim back as needed.

TEMPERATURE: Average temperatures. See care tips 55–57.

WATER: Likes to be moist at all times. See care tips 21 and 22.

HUMIDITY: Likes extra humidity. Mist often. See care tips 31–37.

FOOD: Seldom needs fertilizer but can benefit from a very mild solution every few waterings.

SOIL: A good potting soil with moisture-retaining ingredients is best. Plants are best repotted in spring when necessary; smaller plants can be easily made from a larger plant. See 4 below and care tips 80–84.

PESTS AND PROBLEMS: Rare.

TIP: This plant was always considered a ground-cover for outdoor use before it was considered a houseplant and can be used as such around the base of other houseplants. See 5 below and arranging tip 11.

MEANING: This plant is also known as the "Cor-sican curse," because it spreads rapidly and can be invasive. In Corsica it can be found in cracks in every wall, between stepping-stones, and so on. This plant is traditionally sent as a gift but to relay the message "Mind your own business."

1. Baby tears (opposite) produce soft mounds of small, delicate, oval green leaves that form clumps of glossy foliage.

2. The angel tears plant is a smaller version of baby tears with very tiny leaves.

3. New plants are easily made by gently tearing sections away from the established plant. Pot these pieces in small containers, and new plants will soon become established.

4. This plant can be placed around the base of other house-plants that have similar light and water requirements and offers an attractive way to add humidity. See arranging tip 11.

5. Baby tears are charming when planted alone in little pots.

6. Nertera depressa (or granadensis) is a close relative of baby tears but is covered with small, shiny orange berries. The plant has small, white flowers in the spring and in the fall develops berries, which it keeps for a few months. This plant is usually discarded after the berries are finished.

NAME: Foliage begonia, rex begonia.

VARIETIES: There are more than 1,000 species, with countless hybrids and variations, many of them grown for their brilliant leaves and others for their beautiful flowers. The most popular and striking of the foliage begonias for houseplant use are the rex varieties.

SEASON: Available all year.

COLOR: Various patterns and combinations of greens, reds, pink, copper, burgundy, black, and silver.

SCENT: None.

LIGHT: Bright, but no direct sun. See care tip 41. A copper color on the leaves may indicate too much light.

TEMPERATURE: Between 65° and 75°F during the day and 55° and 65°F at night. Begonias will be unhappy if they are too hot or too cold.

WATER: Keep the soil evenly moist, allowing it to dry only slightly before watering. See care tips 21 and 22.

HUMIDITY: High. Browning leaf tips and margins may indicate a need for higher humidity. See care tips 31–38. Be careful of misting, and allow for proper airflow. See care tips 19, 38, and 51. These plants always benefit from the double-potting method. See container tip 11.

FOOD: Feed every two weeks during growing season with a weak solution of balanced liquid fertilizer. See care tip 70.

SOIL: Soil with good draining qualities is a must, as begonias need a lot of air in the soil. See care tip 52.

PROPAGATION: Leaf cuttings. See care tip 86.

PESTS AND PROBLEMS: Mealy bugs. See care tip 110. Begonias readily develop a powdery mildew, which is indicated by a gray, dusty appearance on the leaves caused by a humid, stagnant environment. See care tip 38. Always allow for proper air circulation. See care tip 51.

TIP: Begonias tend to be leggy. Pinch the tip of branches to promote lateral growth. See care tip 95. At desired fullness, stop pinching to allow the plant to grow.

MEANING: Beware; warning; dark thoughts.

NOTE: These plants usually last only about a year or two, so don't expect them to become a permanent accessory in your home.

1. Rex begonias or foliage begonias are grown for their showy leaves, and the colored patterns and metallic markings make them very desirable as indoor plants. The leaves are streaked, bordered, spotted, and splotched by many colors of vibrant shades. Leaf size, shape, and texture are also varied and include heart, star, diamond, and oval shapes; textures include waxy and smooth, dull and puckered, and wavy. Foliage begonias can have a bushy or trailing habit and may flower in midwinter to late spring, although the flowers are insignificant and should be removed.

Some striking foliage begonia varieties are:

2a. The Cleopatra variety looks like a mound of maple leaves in fall.

2b. The unusual escargot begonia with its snail-like leaves.

2c. The showy iron cross variety with the dark bold markings within the chartreuse green-colored leaves.

3. (opposite) Angel-wing begonias are also wonderful plants for an indoor foliage and blooming option. The delightful name comes from their beautiful wing-shaped leaves, which bear speckles, spots, ruffles, or stripes in many patterns and colors. Their foliage is lush and full, and if conditions are favorable, lovely, delicate blossoms will appear in colors of light peach and pale pink to almost red and may continue to bloom all year long.

4. To select a healthy begonia, look for a full plant with signs of new growth at the base and some healthy mature leaves. Begonias tend to have brittle stems, so watch for damaged branches.

5. Flowering begonias are also popular house and garden plants. The two most popular are the tuberous and the reiger varieties. Flowering begonias have lush clusters of flowers that resemble roses with showy waxy single or double blooms. These plants often bloom for months and provide a brilliant show. Tuberous begonias are mostly sold as outside container plants but will do well indoors in the right conditions. They bloom in light shade outdoors and in bright light indoors. They go dormant after flowering, usually in winter, but the tubers can be saved and replanted the following season. After they flower, allow the plants to dry until the foliage dies back, remove the foliage and store the tubers in a cool, dark dry location until spring to replant for another season. The tubers, which look like little sweet potatoes, should be firm with no soft spots; plant them to three inches deep, cup-side up, in well-drained soil, and keep them evenly moist.

Reiger, or elatior, begonias are closely related to tuberous begonias and require the same growing conditions but may flower for several months at a time and are available all year. However, reiger begonias are very difficult to bring into flower again and should be considered a temporary color display; it is best to discard the plant after the flowering period.

6. Nothing beats flowering begonias for adding a dramatic splash of color to your windowsill or coffee table. Creating a basket full of flowering begonias is like splurging on a huge bouquet of roses, but they last for months.

NAME: Bromeliad, air plant.

VARIETIES: The bromeliad family has more than 2,700 species, and many varieties are commonly available or can be used as houseplants with wide variations in both foliage and flowers.

SEASON: Available all year.

COLOR: Various shades of white, yellow, green, pink, orange, red, gray, and deeper burgundy and brown shades. The leaves range from grasslike to straplike and can be spotted or striped.

SCENT: None.

LIGHT: Bright, indirect light, although they can tolerate lower light for very long periods. A yellowish or pale-green plant may indicate too much light.

TEMPERATURE: Bromeliads do best at 70° to 75°F during the day and 60° to 65°F at night. Cool evenings encourage more color.

WATER: Most bromeliads have a cup; see 2 below. Also keep the soil lightly moist at all times. See care tips 16–18.

HUMIDITY: High. See care tips 31–37.

FOOD: Bromeliads do not need fertilizer but benefit from light applications when actively growing. Occasionally spritz the leaves with a weak solution of fertilizer and water, or sprinkle a little slow-release fertilizer on the soil.

SOIL: Bromeliads naturally grow above the ground, attaching their roots to trunks and branches of trees. Therefore, these plants cannot tolerate heavy soil. A coarse mix of bark chips added to a porous potting mix will provide plenty of air and drainage for the roots. See care tip 65. Do not pot these plants too deeply; the bottom leaves should be at or slightly above soil level. Plants may have to be staked to maintain stability until they are well rooted. See care tip 100.

PROPAGATION: Bromeliads flower only once. Then new plants, called "pups," usually sprout around the base of the plant. See care tips 84 and 88.

PESTS AND PROBLEMS: Occasional problems with scale or mealy bugs. See care tip 110.

TIP: It is very important to keep bromeliad foliage clean and dust free, because the plants have water-absorbing scales on the surface of their leaves. See care tips 90 and 92.

NOTE: The best-known bromeliad is the pineapple.

1. Bromeliads are fascinating plants with numerous variations in size, shape, and color. The flowering part of the plant comprises brilliantly colored stalks, or bracts, from which flowers emerge. The stalks may be separated, large, and leaflike or they may overlap to form dense spikes. Blooms are short-lived, but the stalks remain for months.

2. Bromeliad foliage is usually arranged in a rosette or cup of overlapping leaves, a water-holding reservoir. Most bromeliads absorb water and minerals through their leaves and cups, so always keep the cup filled. Empty and flush it out once a month.

3. Bromeliads adapt easily to growing conditions indoors and are colorful and dramatic as houseplants. Because they can tolerate low-light situations, they make a perfect design touch for any location.

5a

5b

7

5c

6

4. (no photo) Some bromeliads bloom easily; others do not. Give your plant more light and increase the temperature to encourage flowering. Bromeliads can be induced to flower by exposure to ethylene gas. The home gardener can place a healthy, mature plant, with all the water drained from its cup, inside a tightly closed clear plastic bag for about a week with a ripe apple, which releases ethylene gas as it ages. When the plant is removed, the flowers should appear within six to fourteen weeks.

Some popular bromeliads are:

5a. Aechmea (silver urn plant) is the most familiar bromeliad. This variety has stiff, wide, arching leaves with silver bands and a bold, pink, conelike flower stalk.

5b. Vriesia has molted or banded foliage with showy arrow-like flowers, usually in shades of red, yellow, and orange.

5c. Cryptanthus (earth star) is low-growing and resembles a starfish. The solid, striped, or banded leaves may be white, green, brown, bronze, silver, pink, or red; the flowers are usually inconspicuous.

5d. (opposite) Guzmania has soft, green leaves, sometimes striped or banded, with showy flower stalks in flamboyant colors. The most common guzmania is the bright red scarlet star, but the torchlike flower stalks are available in several colors.

6. Most air plants have insignificant flowers, but the tillandsia variety, commonly known as the blue-flowered torch, has gray-green grassy foliage and brilliant pink flower stalks with bright purple blooms. See number 3, page 76.

7. Bromeliads are known as "air plants" because they take in all necessary moisture and nutrients from the air and do not need to be anchored in a soil mix. The plants are mostly silver in color like this xerographica, owing to the large number of reflective nutrient- and water-absorbing scales on their leaves. The most common air plant is Spanish moss. Air plants must be misted daily and should be soaked every two weeks for a couple of hours.

NAME: Cactus.

VARIETIES: More than 2,500 varieties, with two main types, the desert and the forest varieties.

SEASON: Available all year.

COLOR: Mostly green to gray-green, with varying colors of thorns and coverings. Flowers range from fuchsia, pinks, yellow, white, pale green, and orange.

SCENT: A few unusual fragrant varieties, but most have no scent.

LIGHT: Desert types require high light and the forest types prefer medium light. See care tip 41.

TEMPERATURE: Most will do fine in the average home but traditionally like it hot in the spring and summer with a cooling period in the winter (45° to 55°F) to encourage the formation of flower buds.

WATER: Cactus plants are succulents. See care tip 14. Do not wet the body of the cactus or let the pot stand in water; both situations can cause rot. See care tips 20–22.

HUMIDITY: Low humidity is fine for the desert types, but good ventilation is essential. The forest types prefer moderate to high humidity. See care tips 31–37.

FOOD: Feed in very small amounts and only during the growing season. Pellet or time-release fertilizers are good for cacti and can last for the entire season. Apply once in the spring, making sure to use a low-nitrogen option. See care tips 70 and 74c.

SOIL: Use the mixes designed for desert cactus, or mix equal parts soil and sand. Desert types need repotting only every three to five years. Transplant into dry soil and a dry pot, and wait a week before watering to establish the roots and avoid rot. Forest cacti use regular potting soil and usually need repotting every three years. See care tip 83.

PESTS AND PROBLEMS: Scale and mealy bugs. See care tip 110. If plants are watered from above or if soil is waterlogged, the base of the cactus will become discolored, soft, and mushy. See care tips 20–22.

TIP: During the summer, cacti appreciate being moved outdoors for bright light and breezes during the day and cooler nights. See care tip 54. The forest types prefer the shade outside in summer. Bring them indoors in the early fall before frost.

NOTE: Prickly-pear cactus juice is used to treat many ailments, from diabetes to hangovers. Edible parts are commonly used in Mexican cuisine.

1. Cacti make up a striking and diversified plant group, and most types will work as houseplants. They are easy to grow and come in many shapes, sizes, colors, and flowering habits. Cacti have thick, fleshy, green stems and most have thorns or needles or are covered with hairlike fibers. Colorful flowers are a bonus.

2. Commonly used with Southwestern decor, a cactus can provide an unexpected, whimsical addition to any interior. This plain farmhouse setting welcomes the unusual texture and form this cactus adds to the room.

3a

3d

3b

4

3c

Some of the most popular desert cacti are:

3a. Echinocactus varieties (barrel cacti) are ball-shaped plants with ferocious thorns. The showy golden barrel is the best known.

3b. Opuntia varieties include the prickly pears, sometimes called bunny ears, which have large, flattened pads jointed together and covered with tufts of thorns, and the chollas, which have more cylindrical segments.

3c. Parodia varieties (ball cacti) are round and squat.

3d. Cereus varieties are large columnar plants; some older plants have branches. Best known is the saguaro cactus (Cereus giganteus) of Arizona and Mexico, the symbol of deserts in the Southwest. Some of the cereus varieties have exquisite nocturnal blooms and fragrance.

4. Among forest-type cacti, the schlumbergera varieties are commonly known as the Christmas or Easter cacti; they have dark-green, flattened, and segmented stems that arch gracefully over the edges of their containers. Showy, lush flowers bloom from the stem tips when days are cooler and shorter. After a summer outdoors, new growth should be visible on the stem tips. Stop fertilizing and water less, and put the plant in a cool place for at least twelve to four-teen hours of uninterrupted darkness a day. When flower buds appear, begin to give the plant regular water and wait for the spectacular show! Repeat this process every year to trigger blooms.

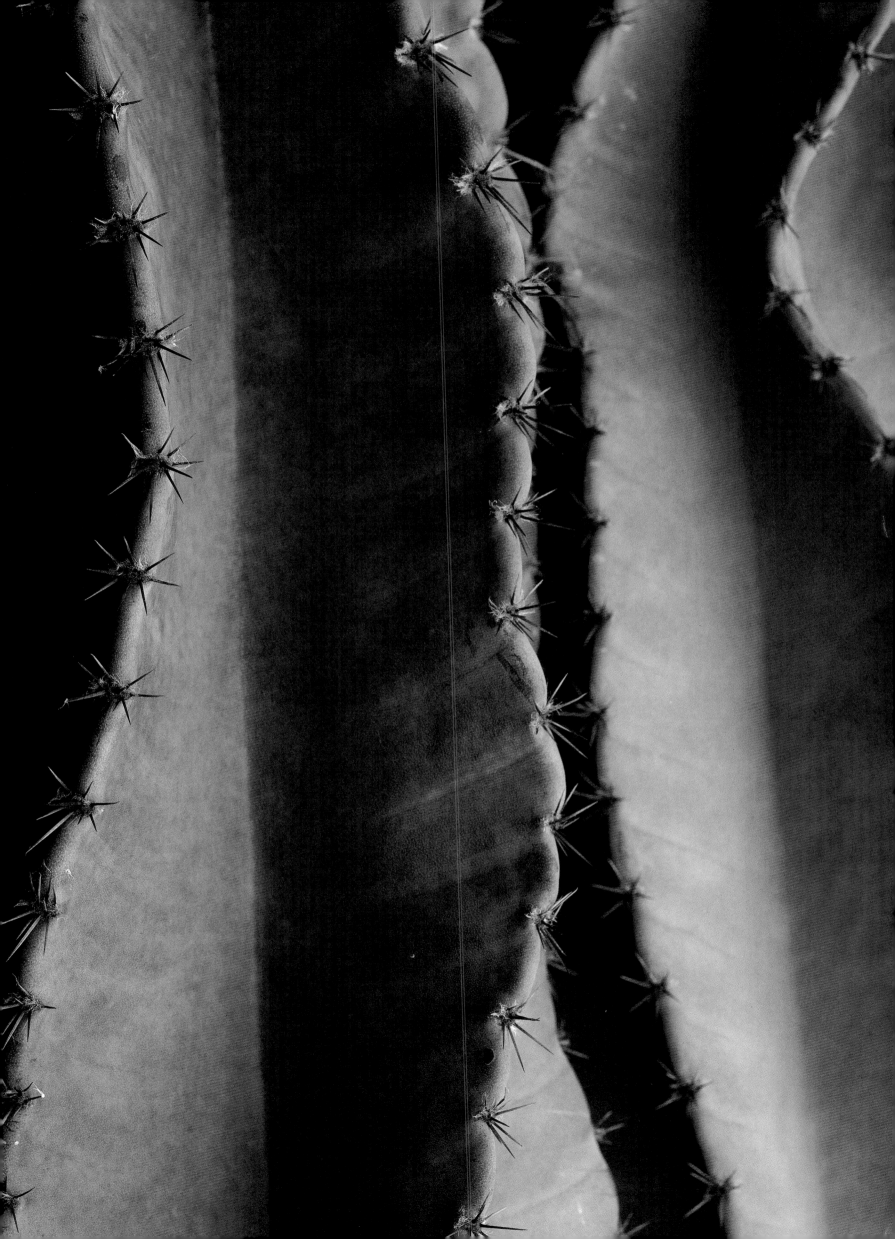

NAME: Cast iron plant, aspidistra.

VARIETIES: Aspidistra elatior varieties.

SEASON: Available all year.

COLOR: Solid deep-green leaves are most common; some varieties have stripes and speckles.

SCENT: None.

LIGHT: Medium light. See care tip 41. Also grows just fine in low light; the leaves may fade in too much light.

TEMPERATURE: Will tolerate a wide range, but average temperatures are ideal. See care tips 55–57. Aspidistra is an ideal plant for a cool area of your house.

WATER: Evenly moist is ideal, although the plant will survive with less water. Also likes a shower now and then. See care tip 92.

HUMIDITY: This plant likes some humidity but does not require it.

FOOD: Fertilize every three to four months in low light conditions and monthly at higher light levels during the growing season.

SOIL: Any good-quality potting soil is fine. This plant is a very slow grower and needs to be repotted only every three to four years.

PESTS AND PROBLEMS: Generally pest free.

TIP: The aspidistra is a perfect plant for indoors. It is one of the easiest plants to grow and is virtually indestructible. Because it is slow-growing, it is usually expensive, but it offers long-term enjoyment and beauty. Remove any brown-spotted foliage to keep the plant attractive and to encourage new growth. This plant likes to spend the summer outdoors in the shade.

MEANING: The common name, cast iron plant, comes from the plant's ability to tolerate poor conditions, such as low light, drafts, cold or hot temperatures, infrequent watering, and dust accumulation while it remains pest-free, as if it were made of cast iron.

NOTE: This is one of the few plants that helped inspire a book title, George Orwell's 1936 novel *Keep the Aspidistra Flying*.

1. The dark-green, leathery leaves grow two to three feet long and make a striking addition to any setting. The plant occasionally produces groups of purplish-brown flowers at ground level near the base of the leaves. Purchase plants with big, healthy leaves and good color. See care tip 1. Check the base of the plant for new growth, as there should be new leaf tips peaking through the soil.

2a, 2b. The variegated and spotted varieties require more work than the solid green plant, because they need more light and proper watering to maintain the color; the plants soon revert to plain green leaves without it. See care tips 21, 22, and 47.

3. With its high tolerance for poor growing conditions, this is the best choice for that difficult area of your house. The simple, striking large green leaves add a little life to an otherwise dull spot.

4. These beautiful leaves make a great addition to cut flower arrangements, accenting the flowers and holding them in place; the foliage often lasts for months when cut and looks stunning alone in a vase when the flowers fade. See arranging tip 17.

NAME: Coleus, rainbow plant, painted nettle.
VARIETIES: About 500 varieties of coleus are in cultivation, and all can be grown as houseplants.
SEASON: Available spring through autumn.
COLOR: Foliage colors range through a multitude of hues, including yellow, red, burgundy, crimson, pink, green, chartreuse, orange, cream, brown, and black, with every combination imaginable.
SCENT: A member of the mint family, coleus can have a slightly spicy, musky scent.
LIGHT: Bright light. See care tip 41. Leaf drop is common if the plants do not get enough sunlight.
TEMPERATURE: Performs best between 70° and 85°F and will not tolerate cold.
WATER: Coleus requires lots of water, so keep evenly moist at all times but never soggy. See care tips 21 and 22.
HUMIDITY: High. See care tips 31–38.
FOOD: Feed twice a month with a diluted solution during the growing season. See care tip 74a.
SOIL: Coleus should be planted in a light, quick-draining potting soil.
PESTS AND PROBLEMS: Mealy bugs, aphids, and white fly infestations are common. See care tip 110.
TIP: Older plants tend to become leggy, and the foliage color fades over time. For a healthy, rejuvenated plant, take a cutting from the stem just below a group of leaves with a clean, sharp knife. See care tip 87.

1. Coleus plants are best known for their bright colors and vast variety of foliage forms. They are most often used as container plants outdoors in summer but are also nice houseplants so long as they receive sufficient light and food. Coleus plants are very easy to grow.

2. Coleus flowers are barely noticeable. By removing the flower spikes and keeping the plant pinched back, the plant can be kept in a growing state for several seasons. Pinch off flowers as soon as they develop to prevent the plant from producing seeds. Once a coleus is allowed to go to seed, it has completed its life cycle and will usually die. Pinching is also necessary to prevent leggy growth. See care tip 95. Coleus is very durable, so you can cut and pinch your plant back severely if needed.

With deeply cut leaves, unusual patterns, and psychedelic colors, coleus offer many possibilities as houseplants:

3a. Bright lime green with chocolate brown patches.

3b. Brilliant shades of sunset orange.

3c. Pair almost any variety with another to create your own combination.

Also see Gloxinia.

NAME: Codiaeum, croton, variegated laurel, Joseph's coat.

VARIETIES: Codiaeum variegatum.

SEASON: Available all year.

COLOR: Leaf colors range from solid to variegated and patterned, from almost black to browns, yellows, crimson, pinks, oranges, greens, cream, and white.

SCENT: None.

LIGHT: Bright light. See care tip 41. Bright light intensifies color and variegation in the leaves; low light diminishes it.

TEMPERATURE: Around 75°F during the day, 55° to 60° at night. Avoid temperatures below 60° and cold drafts, as leaves will drop. Croton does not perform at its best when temperatures are too warm.

WATER: Keep moist at all times during spring and summer months; in winter, allow the soil surface to dry slightly before watering. Leaves may drop if soil dries out completely. See care tips 16–18, 21, and 22.

HUMIDITY: High. See care tips 31–37. Insufficient humidity can cause leaf drop. Foliage should be misted at least two to three times a week; this also helps maintain the natural shine.

FOOD: Feed monthly from late spring through summer, and not at all in winter. Overfertilization can cause leaf drop.

SOIL: Use a moisture-retaining potting mix, since crotons do not like to dry out. They like to be somewhat crowded in their containers, so repot only when needed. See care tips 80–83.

PESTS AND PROBLEMS: Scale and spider mites. See care tip 110.

TIP: Leaf drop is very common with croton plants and may have several causes, but since this finicky plant needs a period of acclimatization in a new environment, don't worry if your plant drops a few leaves and loses its shine after a few days. Provide the right growing conditions and be patient; the croton will soon regain its vigor. Also see arranging tip 17.

NOTE: Poisonous. See care tip 6. Always wear gloves when handling this plant, as the sap in the leaves can irritate skin and stain clothes. Recent research indicates that oil from the croton plant may be useful in treating certain types of cancer.

1. Few houseplants are available with such great colors and shapes, hence the nickname "Joseph's coat." Leaves are glossy and leathery in texture and may be wide or narrow, flat, twisted, or curled; patterns include spots, stripes, streaks, and blotches.

2. Since leaf drop is common in croton plants, check the lower branches for full, healthy growth when purchasing a plant. The leaves should be slightly upright and firm. Shake the plant gently to see if any foliage drops. See care tip 1.

3. The small speckled leaf variety, Croton aucubifolium, brightens up this breakfast nook.

4. These truly striking plants make a real contribution to any interior. A few crotons indoors can color your world.

NAME: Cyclamen.

VARIETIES: Persicum varieties are available in large, intermediate, and miniature flowering types with single, double, and ruffled blooms.

SEASON: Available fall through spring.

COLOR: Whites, lavender, purple, salmon, pinks, magenta, and red flowers with some two-tone and variegated varieties. Leaves are marbled green, silver, gray, and bronze.

SCENT: None.

LIGHT: Bright light, no direct sun. See care tip 41.

TEMPERATURE: Cyclamen like cool temperatures (50° to 60°F) and will not perform well in a warm location.

WATER: Cyclamen must be evenly moist and never allowed to dry out. Water daily if necessary, but let the plant drink for only ten minutes at a time. You may water from the top but only around the edge of the pot and very slowly. See care tips 16–18. This plant grows from a corm about four to six inches in size and concave in shape, and it will rot if it absorbs too much water or if water is poured directly into the center of the plant. See care tips 20–22.

HUMIDITY: Medium to high. See care tips 31–37. Cyclamen benefit from good air circulation; a stagnant, humid environment can cause the plants to rot. See care tips 51 and 52.

FOOD: Newly purchased cyclamen will not need fertilizing for about a month. Then begin feeding your plant with a very weak solution every two weeks through flowering time. See "Care after Flowering" below. See care tips 71–74a.

SOIL: Cyclamen prefer a lightweight potting mix with some added sand to help drain excess moisture from the corm. See care tip 65.

PESTS AND PROBLEMS: Aphids and spider mites. See care tip 110. Cyclamen mites, indicated by twisted, stunted leaves, can also be a problem. These bugs are so tiny they resemble a thin layer of dust. See care tips 106, 108, and 109. Most pest sprays do not eliminate cyclamen mites.

TIP: Always pinch spent flowers and leaves at the base of the plant to encourage new growth and a longer flowering time.

MEANING: Cyclamen are said to bring fertility, happiness, protection, and lust!

NOTE: Poisonous. See care tip 6.

CARE AFTER FLOWERING: After flowering, gradually reduce watering to encourage the leaves to yellow and die back. Once the plant is bare, let the soil dry completely. Put plant in a cool, dark space and water sparingly, or bury the pot in a shady part of the garden and allow it to rest during the warm months. In cooler weather, plant the corm in new potting soil, leaving one-third exposed. Put in indirect light and wait for new growth. Begin watering again and feeding with a very weak solution every two weeks throughout the flowering time. Cyclamen plants can be enjoyed for many years.

1. Cyclamen are charming plants with a beautiful cluster of heart-shaped leaves below a crown of delicate, nodding flowers that resemble butterflies in flight.

2a, 2b. Buy cyclamen with a few open flowers and many buds and new leaves. Check the base of the plant for new growth. The leaves and flowers should be firm and upright. Blooms can last up to four months. Yellowing leaves, dried edges, limited signs of new growth, and flimsy leaves indicate the plant was dried out, overwatered, or exposed to warm conditions. A dried-out cyclamen rarely recovers its full potential.

3. Cyclamen plants provide lasting color throughout the winter and spring, a perfect substitute for cut flowers. They are also ideal for holiday displays and last much longer than poinsettias. See arranging tips 5 and 19.

NAME: Dumb cane, dieffenbachia.

VARIETIES: This group comprises about 30 varieties, from which many hybrids have been developed. The most common varieties are the Dieffenbachia amoena, D. oerstedii, and D. picta.

SEASON: Available all year.

COLOR: All shades of green with yellow, light green, cream, and white markings or spots.

SCENT: None.

LIGHT: Medium to bright light, but no direct sun, See care tip 41. Plants can withstand low light conditions for extended periods of time.

TEMPERATURE: Average to warm temperatures, 70° to 80°F during the day, 60° to 65° at night, and never below 55°. Will not tolerate cold drafts.

WATER: Allow soil to become moderately dry before watering, but then soak thoroughly. See care tips 21 and 22.

HUMIDITY: High. See care tips 31–37.

FOOD: Feed monthly during spring and summer, every two months in the winter. See care tips 69–79.

SOIL: Use a rich soil mix with good draining qualities. Plants can be repotted at any time of the year. See care tips 80–83.

PESTS AND PROBLEMS: Spider mites, aphids, and mealy bugs. See care tip 110. Dust quickly accumulates on the leaves, so clean often. See care tips 89–92.

TIP: As the plant grows, the lower leaves drop and the canelike stem becomes visible. A plant that is too tall and leggy may be cut back to any height; a new set of leaves will sprout at the top of the cut stem. The cut portion will develop roots in soil or water and may be planted in the original pot. See care tip 87. This creates a fuller plant with a more layered look and is best done in spring or early summer. See also Dracaena number 2.

MEANING: The name "dumb cane" refers to what happens when the plant is ingested: The throat closes up and the person cannot speak. Dumb cane was used in medieval times to keep disorderly folk from speaking their minds.

NOTE: This is one of the best plants for purifying indoor air, but all parts of the plant are poisonous. Always use gloves when handling. See care tip 6.

1. Dieffenbachias are tropical plants with large, lush leaves that are oval with pointed tips. Colors include dark or medium green with cream, light green, yellowish, or white markings. Plants may reach four to six feet in height.

A healthy dieffenbachia should have strong, clean leaves growing out of sturdy stems. Small plants usually are sold with a single stem; larger, more mature plants may have multiple stems. Some common varieties are:

2a. Dieffenbachia amoena 'Tropic Snow', the most common variety, has bright green edges and creamy margins.

2b. D. picta 'Exotica' (leopard lily) is marked with spots and speckles.

3. The striking white leaves of another picta variety, 'Camilla', will light up any corner of a room.

NAME: Dracaena.

VARIETIES: The most common varieties for houseplant use are Dracaena fragrans, marginata, deremensis, and reflexa.

SEASON: Available all year.

COLOR: Solid green or striped with green, white, cream, and yellow; some have burgundy or magenta stripes.

SCENT: None.

LIGHT: Medium to bright, filtered light is best, but will do fine in low light. See care tip 41. The vivid coloring in the leaves will fade and may revert to green in lower light over time.

TEMPERATURE: Average temperatures. See care tips 55–57.

WATER: Let dry slightly before watering. Dracaenas are very sensitive to fluoride. See care tips 16–18. Symptoms include yellowed tips or leaf margins and scorched areas. Water less in winter, but never allow plant to dry out completely.

HUMIDITY: High. Brown leaf tips result from dry air. See care tips 31–37.

FOOD: Feed lightly once in spring. Leaf tips and margins may burn or yellow if fertilized too often.

SOIL: Use a commercial houseplant mix, but avoid one with a high percentage of perlite, which contains fluoride. Slow-growing dracaenas like to be slightly root-bound, so repot only every two to three years in spring.

PESTS AND PROBLEMS: Scale and spider mites. See care tip 110. Brown or yellow leaf tips are commonly caused by tap water, perlite, overfeeding, and low humidity.

TIP: It is natural for the lower leaves to yellow and fall off, so remove spent leaves to maintain appearance. See number 2 below.

MEANING: *Dracaena* is the Greek word for female dragon and is symbolic of power and protection.

NOTE: Dracaenas are effective indoor pollution fighters, especially for formaldehyde.

1b. D. deremensis (ribbon plant), the smallest species. The most common variety is the solid green, but the most colorful is the "lemon-lime."

1c. D. fragrans (corn plant) with thick stems and long, slender leaves that resemble sweet corn.

2. These plants expose more of their stems with age. A plant that is too tall and leggy may be cut back to any height; a new set of leaves will sprout at the top of the cut stem. The cut portion will develop roots in soil or water and may be planted in the original pot. See care tip 87. This creates a fuller plant with a layered look and is best done in spring or early summer. Also see Dieffenbachia "Tip."

3. "Lucky bamboo" is not a bamboo but a dracaena (the sanderia variety), which is considered very lucky in feng shui. Select a plant with three or eight stalks (lucky numbers), plant in pebbles, and grow in bright, indirect light. Add water when necessary and change it once a month. Lucky bamboo can last for years with proper care and, because it is believed to enhance prosperity, makes the perfect housewarming gift.

4. The marginata variety is like a sculpture with smooth, gray stems that bend and twist artistically as they grow toward the light.

Dracaenas have straplike foliage, which is colorfully striped, often with showy bicolor and tricolor combinations. One common variety for houseplant use is (opposite) Dracaena reflexa (song of India), with its spiraling rosettes of yellow and green striping.

1a. D. marginata (dragon tree), with gray stems topped by clusters of slender, arching leaves. This variety may have magenta in its stripes.

1a

1b

1c

1d

1e

NAME: Fern.

VARIETIES: There are about 9,000 species of fern, many of them suitable as houseplants.

COLOR: All shades from light green to deep forest green. Ferns may be striped with white or silver or tinged with tones from red to burgundy.

SCENT: None.

LIGHT: Although known as shade-loving plants, ferns require bright light indoors, but without direct sunlight. A window facing east or north is ideal. See care tip 41.

TEMPERATURE: Ferns do best at 60° to 70°F and may suffer in very warm conditions. Keep away from drafts and heat sources.

WATER: Keep moist at all times, but don't let ferns stand in water. See care tips 21 and 22.

HUMIDITY: High. Ferns must have moist air to flourish or their fronds will become dry and brown. See care tips 31–37.

FOOD: Feed every two weeks with a diluted solution during the growing season and once every two months in winter.

SOIL: Use a loose, nutrient-rich, moisture-retaining potting mix. Repot at least once a year, in the spring. If ferns grow from a crown or an exposed rhizome (see bird's-nest fern, 1c below, as an example), do not bury these below the soil surface. See care tip 83.

PESTS AND PROBLEMS: Ferns are prone to scale. See care tip 110. Some mature ferns will develop spores (seeds) on the undersides of their leaves, but these should not be mistaken for scale. If the brown dots are uniform, they are spores; if they are irregular, your plant is probably infected with scale.

TIP: All ferns welcome a summer in the garden in a sheltered spot. See care tip 54.

NOTE: Ferns are among the oldest plants on earth, having been around for more than 300 million years, and they have changed very little over time. Only algae and mosses are older.

MEANING: Fascination, sincerity, magic.

Ferns are great for outdoor and indoor gardening, but only a few varieties are available as houseplants. They range in size from the tiny button fern to the large Boston fern. Some common houseplant varieties include:

1a. The sword fern varieties (nephrolepis) include the Boston fern, best known for its slender fronds, or leaves, that grow one to two feet long (and up to five feet). Give this fern plenty of elbow room as the long fronds are easily damaged from contact.

1b. The maidenhair fern (adiantum var.) is one of the prettiest ferns but the most difficult to grow. The thin stems range from chocolate to almost black, and the delicate, lacy leaves are bright green. The key to success is a very moist atmosphere. Do not allow this variety to dry out.

1c. The bird's-nest fern (asplenium var.) has wide, flat, waxy, chartreuse fronds with wavy edges that grow around a deep-brown fibrous crown, which resembles a nest. The young fronds look like green eggs when they first appear.

1d. Ribbon ferns (pteris var.) have deeply divided green fronds with slender serrated leaflets of green with white or light-green variations that resemble ribbons.

1e. The button fern (pellaea) is solid green with small, round shiny leaflets along the arching fronds.

1f. Hare's-foot ferns have visible, furry root systems (rhizomes) that resemble a rabbit's foot. Two varieties share this nickname. The polypodium varieties have larger, waxy leaves, usually bluish-green in color; fronds of the davallia varieties resemble a carrot top. See number 4 below.

1g. The stag-horn fern (Platycerium bifurcatum) has large, spectacular fronds divided at the tips and resembling deer antlers. In nature this type of fern grows high up on tree trunks. As a houseplant, it is commonly grown in hanging baskets or attached to a piece of wood. The best way to water this fern is to plunge the entire plant into a bucket of water and allow it to drain completely before hanging it again.

2. The asparagus fern is not actually a fern but is commonly called one because of its feathery stems. The care is basically the same as for ferns, but the plant is a little more tolerant. Remove any yellowing leaves so the plant will make new growth.

3. Fronds vary greatly in size—from tree ferns with their 21-foot fronds to tiny specimen ferns with fronds only 1/16 inch long. Fern fronds are fragile and tender, and if the tip is damaged, the frond will die. Ferns keep their tips curled until the last moment to protect them. Crowding or brushing against objects or other plants may cause them to turn brown, so give them plenty of elbow room.

4. Rhizomes are the root system from which the fronds grow. Most rhizomes are inconspicuous or underground, but in some species, such as the rabbit's-foot fern, the rhizome is visible. To be sure the plant is healthy, check often for new growth arising from the crown or the rhizomes.

5. Since most ferns demand a humid environment, they do well in a terrarium environment. These bird's-nest ferns look beautiful buried in moss in the glass vessel. See container tip 6.

6. The beautiful color, shape, and texture of ferns can add a soothing touch to an interior setting.

1a

1b

NAME: Ficus, fig, ornamental fig.

VARIETIES: The diverse ficus, or fig, family has more than 800 species and thousands of varieties, of which several are desirable houseplants. Although related to the edible fruit-bearing fig tree, the interior varieties are referred to as ornamental figs and can be trees, shrubs, or vines.

SEASON: Available all year.

COLOR: Mostly shades of green, but some have variegated foliage.

SCENT: None.

LIGHT: Bright light to medium light, but not direct sun for the entire day. See care tip 41.

TEMPERATURE: 75° to 85°F during the day; no lower than 60° at night. Ficus plants are very sensitive to sudden temperature changes. See care tip 53.

WATER: Except for the creeping fig (see 1e, page 102), which should be kept moist at all times, allow ficus plants to dry a bit before watering and then water thoroughly. See care tips 8, 9, 21, and 22. Ficus will use less water during the winter months. The practice of keeping soil too wet or allowing it to get very dry can result in leaf loss.

HUMIDITY: Medium to high. See care tips 31–37.

FOOD: Feed monthly throughout the growing season. Withhold fertilizer in the winter months.

SOIL: Use any good potting mix. Ficus like to be pot-bound, so infrequent repotting is best. Since ficus can be rapid growers, their size can be controlled by root pruning and putting them back into the same pot. See care tip 83.

PESTS AND PROBLEMS: Scale, mealy bugs, and spider mites. See care tip 110. Provide plenty of air circulation to help prevent fungus disease, and groom the large leaves a few times a month. See care tips 90–92.

TIP: Ficus plants usually need a period of adjustment in a new environment and do not like to be moved once settled; this usually results in leaf drop. See care tips 3–5. The loss of the lowest leaves is caused by age and is normal, but the continued loss of leaves over time is usually caused by overwatering, drought conditions, low temperatures, too little light, too much fertilizer, or cold drafts.

MEANING: The fig tree is an important symbol in history dating back to Adam and Eve. A fig grown in the home is believed to bring love and fertility.

NOTE: Plant sap can cause dermatitis and allergic reactions. Always use gloves when handling. The sap from the elastica variety is used to make rubber.

Ficus as houseplants offer options from low, creeping vines to full, lush shrubs and large, sculptural trees. The most common ficus plants for interior use are:

1a. The very popular variety F. benjamina (weeping fig) has glossy, slightly wavy leaves and ranges from little tabletop plants to multistemmed shrubs and large trees with straight or braided trunks. These plants are the most notorious for dropping leaves. See "Tip" above. New foliage develops quickly with proper light conditions.

1b. The striking F. lyrata (fiddle-leaf fig) has big, wavy, green, fiddle-shaped leaves.

1d

1e

1c. (opposite) Similar to the weeping fig is F. alii, which resembles a willow tree. Its long narrow leaves are not as prone to drop.

1d. F. elastica (rubber tree) has big, glossy, oval leaves, rich green on top and coppery and feltlike underneath. New leaf growth is encased in a red covering that falls off as the leaf unfurls. Variegated as well as burgundy and green colored versions of this old-fashioned favorite are also available. This plant requires a little less water than other ficus varieties and does best in medium light.

1e. F. pumila (creeping fig) has small, leathery, dark green leaves about an inch long. A variegated variety is also available. This fast-growing plant can climb and cling to walls just like ivy. Keep soil moist at all times, as these plants dry out quickly.

2. (no photo) Ficus can be fast growers and, left to their own devices, bush plants can reach up to six feet tall and trees can reach a height of twenty feet or more. The size may be controlled by pruning, which tends to encourage branching and fuller growth. Prune as you would any woody plant: Make your cuts just above a node, where a leaf is attached to the stem, or where another stem branches off. New growth should arise from the pruned areas.

3. If you have the proper space, these creatures of habit make a bold presence in an interior setting.

3

NAME: Fittonia, nerve plant, snakeskin plant, mosaic plant.

VARIETIES: Fittonia verschaffeltii varieties. There are large-leaf plants and smaller dwarf-leaf varieties.

SEASON: Available all year.

COLOR: Light green to deep olive green leaves with a network of red, pink. or white veins.

SCENT: None.

LIGHT: Medium to low light is best. See care tip 41.

TEMPERATURE: Needs constant warm temperatures; 70° to 85°F is ideal. This plant does not tolerate cold temperatures or drafts.

WATER: Keep soil moist at all times; do not let it dry completely. See care tips 8, 16–19, 21, 22, and 24. If the leaves start to shrivel, the soil is too dry. Once the leaves shrivel, they may not revive. See 2 below.

HUMIDITY: High humidity. See care tips 31–37.

FOOD: Feed once a month with a very weak solution during the growing months and not at all in winter.

SOIL: Use any good-draining potting soil and repot each spring. See care tips 80–83.

PESTS AND PROBLEMS: Rare.

TIP: This plant's ideal situation is a terrarium because of its constant need for warmth and high humidity. See container tip 6 and number 3 below. Fittonia plants grown under normal conditions get very leggy and scraggly over time. Keep them pinched back to maintain a full appearance and to promote healthy growth. Insignificant flowers grow on this plant; keep these pinched off as well. See care tips 94–96. Stem cuttings root easily. See care tip 87.

NOTE: The smaller dwarf-leaf varieties are easier to grow than the large-leaf varieties.

1. The charm of fittonia plants comes from the beautiful markings on the dainty, richly colored leaves. The patterns branch intricately like a nerve network.

2. Fittonia plants need constant moisture, so check for water needs almost daily. Once a plant has completely dried out, it is hard to revive. It is best to cut back the damaged foliage and start again. See "Tip" above.

3. A terrarium provides a wonderful, decorative environment with a magical quality. Whatever the container—a pickle jar, fish bowl, or contemporary glass sculpture—you can bring an easily cared-for touch of nature into your home. This rich green and white fittonia is quite beautiful in its glass house. See container tip 6.

1a1

1a2

NAME: Flowering bulbs, forced bulbs.
VARIETIES: The bulbs most commonly forced into premature flowering are amaryllis, paper-white narcissus, muscari, and hyacinth, but many others can be forced, including some varieties of tulips and daffodils. For best results, look for recommended varieties.
SEASON: Late autumn through spring.
COLOR: A wide range is available.
SCENT: Many varieties are fragrant.
LIGHT: Some bulbs require a period of complete darkness coupled with a cooling period to bloom. Put a box or paper bag over potted bulbs for a number of weeks, and then move them into indirect sunlight. After a couple of weeks, when shoots turn green and are four to six inches tall, move the pot to a sunny window to stimulate blooming. When the buds take on color, return them to indirect sunlight so the blossoms last. Some bulbs can be placed directly in bright light to begin their blooming process. Pots must be rotated periodically to insure even growth.
TEMPERATURE: For bulbs that require a cooling period, keep the temperature between 32° and 45°F and allow a gradual transition to warm temperatures after the specified number of weeks, starting in the coolest spot in your house for a week or two before moving to a warmer spot.
WATER: Bulbs planted in soil should be kept evenly moist at all times. For bulbs planted in pebbles or water, always maintain the water at the base of the bulbs. See numbers 2a and 2b, page 108.
HUMIDITY: Average.
FOOD: Not needed, as the bulbs contain everything necessary to bloom.
SOIL: Good drainage is essential as bulbs readily mold and rot. Add equal parts of fine gravel or sand to potting soil. See number 1c, page 108.
PESTS AND PROBLEMS: Pests are uncommon, but bulbs will mold or rot if allowed to rest in water.
TIP: Select the largest bulbs with brown skins intact. Avoid soft or moldy bulbs and be sure they are free from disease and damage. Label each pot with the name of the variety and planting date. Since different varieties require different cooling periods, don't mix different types in the same pot.
NOTE: Most forced bulbs should be discarded after blooming, but some can be planted in the garden and regain their strength to show healthy flowers for the next season or two. Do not force these bulbs again, however, because much of their energy will have been depleted in the forcing process.

Popular flowering bulbs include:

1a1, 1a2. Big, bold amaryllis blooms (1) are very popular at Christmas but can be enjoyed throughout the winter. Amaryllis are available in every color except a true purple, blue, and black; some have double blossoms, and miniature varieties are also available. Plant bulbs in a pot only one to two inches larger in diameter than the bulb; the top half of the bulb should remain exposed (2). Water thoroughly, and do not water again until a sign of new growth appears, then water regularly. Place in a warm, sunny spot until the flower buds develop and then move out of direct sunlight. After blooming, cut off the flowers and stem close to the base of the plant and place plant in the brightest possible location; continue watering as usual. When the foliage starts to brown and wither, place in a dark location, withholding all water and allowing the leaves to die back completely. The bulb may be forced into bloom again after resting for a few months. Remove the upper two inches of soil and top-dress with fresh potting soil; if the pot is not large enough, repot. This cycle may be repeated annually for many years of lovely blossoms. Small plantlets will often develop beside a full-grown amaryllis. Separate them gently from the large bulb and repot them, or leave them attached and allowed to grow to full size along with the original bulb. You could end up with a large pot containing several amaryllis, all blooming at once!

1b. Hyacinth, the fragrant springtime favorite that is most commonly found in blue, purple, pink, and white shades, will require about twelve weeks of cold storage. Hyacinth can be forced in water alone and also in pebbles. When planting hyacinths, you may want to wear gloves, as the skin of the bulb can cause itching and redness.

1c. Paperwhite narcissus are among the most popular and easy-to-force flowers and do not require a cooling period. Paperwhites are very fragrant and most commonly available in pure white, but novelty varieties can be found in cream with touches of yellow and orange. Paperwhites are often potted in shallow containers of gravel but can also be grown in water or in soil. Just place the container in a sunny spot and you'll see roots in a day or so; in three to six weeks you will have beautiful flowers. You can gently scrape the bottom of the bulb to encourage the new roots to sprout and produce blossoms sooner.

1d. (and opposite) Muscari, or grape hyacinth, are charming, fragrant little blossoms in shades of blue and purple and require fourteen to sixteen weeks of cold storage.

The three usual ways to force bulbs are by using pebbles, water, and soil:

2a. Pebbles: Place washed pebbles, gravel, or decorative stones in the bottom of a waterproof bowl or glass container. Settle the base of each bulb into the pebbles until it will stand on its own. Fill container with water up to the base of the bulbs. Hyacinths and narcissus are the best bulbs to force in pebbles and water.

2b. Water: Forcing in water is traditionally done with a glass vase called a "hyacinth glass," which is wider at the top to hold the bulb; any glass vase will work as long as it is wide enough to support the bulb. Fill the container with water up to the base of the bulb. Be sure the bottom of the bulb just touches the water.

2c. Soil: Loosely fill the bottom of a container with two inches or more of potting soil, and put the bulbs in tips up and shoulder to shoulder, so they are slightly touching. Gently add enough potting mix until it covers half the bulb. Water lightly and keep evenly moist at all times.

3. Some bulbs require no cooling period while others need twelve to fifteen weeks. Place pots in a cool, dark spot, such as a retired (but functioning) refrigerator or an unheated garage or basement. See temperature and light requirements above. Keep the soil moist and water levels monitored during the cooling period. After the required number of weeks, check the containers frequently for signs that the bulbs are ready to move—roots growing out of the drainage holes or shoots a few inches tall.

4. If you need to store your bulbs before planting, make sure they get proper ventilation. Store in mesh bags or a paper bag with holes, and nestle them in some moss or shredded paper for protection. If you store bulbs in a refrigerator, do not put them in the same storage bin as fruit, because ripening fruit gives off ethylene gas, which can damage the bulbs. Because some bulbs are poisonous, this storage method is not recommended for households with young children.

5. Spring flowers blooming inside your house during the bleak days of winter can lift your spirits and brighten up your home. Forcing bulbs by mimicking outdoor growing conditions makes it possible for you to have beautiful and often very fragrant spring blossoms in your home weeks before they would normally bloom. The art of persuading bulbs can be quite rewarding, but if this sounds like too much time and work, many bulbs are sold in bloom throughout the winter ready to enjoy immediately.

NAME: Gloxinia.

VARIETIES: The "florist's gloxinia" (Sinningia speciosa) comes in large, standard, and miniature varieties. There are single and double flowering types, with smooth or ruffled petal edges.

SEASON: Available spring and summer.

COLOR: White, pink, red, coral, blue, lavender and purple, or two-tone with white centers or white rims.

SCENT: None.

LIGHT: Bright, indirect light. See care tip 41.

TEMPERATURE: 75° to 85°F during the day; 65° or warmer at night. Low day or night temperatures can delay growth; flowers and leaves will become brittle and break easily. See 3 below. Gloxinias are very sensitive to cold drafts and cold water.

WATER: Keep moist at all times and never let soil dry out, even slightly. Yellow leaves indicate overwatering. See care tips 8, 19–22, and 24.

HUMIDITY: High. See care tips 31–39 and 51.

FOOD: Feed moderately at every watering with a weak solution while buds are developing and flowering.

SOIL: Use a light, well-draining soil mixture, such as an African violet mix. When potting the tuber, make sure that the "hollow" part is on top, very close to the surface. See "Care after Flowering" below.

PESTS AND PROBLEMS: Spider mites. See care tip 110. Tuber rot is caused by waterlogged soil, and leaves and flowers are damaged by water, so do not water the center of the plant.

TIP: One gloxinia can produce well over two dozen flowers. If the first two are pinched off very early, most of the remaining flowers will make a showy display. Remove a few upper leaves to allow light to reach the remaining flower buds.

MEANING: Love at first sight.

NOTE: Gloxinias are sensitive and very difficult to grow. The slightest problem or change in care may disrupt its blooming cycle.

CARE AFTER FLOWERING: After flowering, the plant will go into a resting state. Water less often and then stop watering altogether. Let the leaves die back and let the plant rest for two to four months in the dry soil. Replant the tuberous stem in fresh potting soil and when new growth appears, resume watering.

1. The gloxinia's richly colored bell-shaped blooms are surrounded by large, graceful velvety leaves. The flowers have very deep throats, which offer splendid hues and striking details that contrast beautifully with the petals. Gloxinia is closely related to the African violet.

2. Choose a plant with plenty of unopened buds and healthy leaves. With proper care, the plant will provide spectacular flowers for a month or two.

3. Gloxinia leaves are brittle and can break and tear easily, so surround the plant base with plenty of moist moss to protect the fragile foliage and to supply extra humidity. Gloxinia can be paired with other moisture-loving foliage plants. Here a pretty pink gloxinia is pared with black coleus plants for a striking combination. Also see Coleus.

NAME: Hibiscus.

VARIETIES: Chinese hibiscus, Hibiscus rosa-sinensis.

SEASON: Available summer through fall.

COLOR: Range of wild colors, including reds, pinks, oranges, yellows, bicolors, tricolors, and multicolors in single and double blooms.

SCENT: None.

LIGHT: Bright light. See care tip 41. Turn weekly to encourage uniform growth.

TEMPERATURE: Warm, between 70° and 90°F. Most growth and blooming will stop below 50° until plant warms up again. Temperatures over 95° can cause buds to drop off.

WATER: Hibiscus drink a lot of water but should dry slightly before watering. In summer check for water needs daily; at other times, check twice weekly. Leaves will wilt, yellow, and drop off if the soil dries out completely. See care tips 8, 11, 21, and 22.

HUMIDITY: High. Mist once or twice daily. See care tips 31–37. Curling leaves indicate air is too dry.

FOOD: Feed every week during growing season and monthly in winter, or use a time-release product. See care tip 74c. For the best flowers, use a fertilizer high in potassium. Hibiscus need trace elements and minerals. See care tip 70.

SOIL: Hibiscus roots require air, so use a good-draining potting soil or a soil-less mix and do not pack tightly around the root-ball. See care tip 60. Repot only when absolutely necessary, as hibiscus love to be slightly root-bound. See care tips 80–83. Hibiscus benefit from "pot freshening" in late winter. See care tip 66.

PESTS AND PROBLEMS: Aphids, white flies, and spider mites. See care tip 110. Use insecticidal soap regularly to prevent infestations. Shower or bathe the plant every two months. See care tips 92 and 106.

TIP: Try your hibiscus as a patio plant in the summer. After a short acclimatization period, it will thrive in a partially sunny spot. Remember to bring the plant indoors before the first frost. See care tips 52–54. Hibiscus require annual pruning to maintain shape and size and to stimulate budding, since the plant flowers on new shoots. Prune in early spring: Cut each branch back by one-third to two-thirds of its length; some branches can be removed. Make your cuts below an outward-facing bud or leaf so new shoots will grow away from the trunk. Pinch small plants back to ensure good branching and encourage growth.

MEANING: Delicate beauty.

NOTE: Hibiscus is Hawaii's state flower.

1. Hibiscus are showy tropical flowers with deep-green leaves and large, paperlike trumpet flowers in beautiful vivid colors. Most hibiscus are small shrubs two to three feet high but can grow over six feet. The typical blooming time is summer into fall but hibiscus can bloom year-round. The beautiful flowers last only a day or two.

2. A healthy hibiscus will produce a succession of flower buds for a continuous show.

3. The mesmerizing beauty of hibiscus flowers blooming indoors is a lavish treat.

NAME: Hydrangea.

VARIETIES: Hydrangea macrophylla varieties. Most commonly available as houseplants are the mop-head and lace-cap hydrangeas.

SEASON: Available spring.

COLOR: Pink, red, white, blue, lavender, and purple. Blossom color is determined by alkalinity or acidity of soil. Pink flowers occur when the soil is alkaline. For pink flowers, use one teaspoon of garden lime per quart of water. Beginning in February, drench the plant once every two weeks for four to six applications until flowers develop. Acidic soil results in blue flowers; add aluminum sulfate to the soil (one teaspoon per quart of water). White hydrangeas will remain white regardless of the soil

SCENT: Slightly sweet.

LIGHT: Very bright but filtered light. See care tip 41.

TEMPERATURE: Average temperature. See care tip 55. Blossoms last longer if plant is kept relatively cool, around 60°F.

WATER: Must be moist at all times. Check daily. See care tip 26.

HUMIDITY: High. Do not mist because hydrangeas are prone to mildew, caused by too much humidity. See care tips 19 and 31–37.

FOOD: Newly purchased plants in flower do not need feeding. See care tip 81. See "Care after Flowering" below.

SOIL: Use a nutrient-rich, moisture-retentive potting mix. See care tip 68.

PESTS AND PROBLEMS: Aphids can be a problem in a warm location. See care tip 110.

TIP: Mulch with a layer of damp moss to keep soil moist and to prevent plants from drying out. See care tips 24 and 35. Because many commercial plants are potted in lightweight mix, gently scrape away some loose soil from the top of the pot and replace with an inch of a moisture-retaining mix. See care tip 67.

NOTE: Poisonous. See care tip 6.

CARE AFTER FLOWERING: Cut stems back to half their height. Repot in a slightly larger pot and put outdoors in a cool shady spot or bury the pot in the ground. Water freely through the summer and feed every two weeks. When the weather cools, place the pot in a cool, dark location indoors. Stop feeding in winter, and water just enough to prevent the plant from drying out. In February, put in a bright location and begin a regular watering schedule. When flowers appear, feed every two weeks.

1. Houseplant hydrangeas are dwarf shrubs with big, beautiful, lush leaves and flower heads, which are dense clusters of many individual flowers. The mop-head variety has firm, round flower heads resembling pom-poms. A little green on the flower heads is ideal as this indicates the blossoms are still in the developing stage and your flowers will last longer.

2. The lace-cap variety has flower heads that are flat, round disks of seedlike buds surrounded by a ring of open blossoms.

3. This old-fashioned plant brings a nostalgic feel to formal or informal rooms, like this basket of hydrangeas in a sunny sitting room.

NAME: Ivy.

VARIETIES: The true ivies are the hedera varieties, with hundreds of different types, but many unrelated houseplants are called ivies. The three most common ones include the Swedish ivy (opposite), the grape ivy, and the devil's ivy.

SEASON: Available all year.

COLOR: Endless shades of greens, from bright apple to almost black; some are variegated or bordered with white, creams, yellows, silver, or gray.

SCENT: Most ivies have no scent, but Swedish ivy has a very fragrant, musky, almost licorice scent.

LIGHT: Bright indirect or filtered light, but no direct sun. See care tip 41. Ivies will tolerate low light, but variegated forms may turn all green and plants may become weak and spindly.

TEMPERATURE: Ivy likes to be cool, 65° to 70°F during the day and 50° to 55° at night.

WATER: Water thoroughly; let plant dry somewhat before watering.

HUMIDITY: Moderate. See care tips 31–37.

FOOD: Feed once a month while actively growing. Do not fertilize when plants stop growing, either in the heat of summer or in the winter months.

SOIL: Ivies may be repotted during any season. Any good commercial houseplant potting mix is fine. See care tips 80–83.

PESTS AND PROBLEMS: Spider mites, mealy bugs, aphids, scale, and white flies; spider mites are the most common. See care tip 110. Leaf spots can be caused by a fungus or bacteria. A white dusty coating on the leaves is caused by mildew.

TIP: Many of the problems of growing ivies can be prevented or remedied by periodic baths. See care tip 92. Remove dead and damaged leaves to prevent the spread of pests and disease and to maintain cooler temperatures and proper ventilation. Pinch ivies back to control growth or to retain bushy and healthy growth.

MEANING: Fidelity and marriage.

NOTE: Many hedera varieties are poisonous. See care tip 6. Ivy plants are among the best air purifiers for interior pollutants.

1. Ivies are an incredibly varied group with an amazing range of foliage types. Leaves can be eight inches across or smaller than a dime and range from flat to heart-shaped or triangular; some resemble a bird's foot with narrow lobes and some have curly or ruffled leaves.

2. The English ivy, Hedera helix, is perhaps best known of the true ivies.

3. H. canariensis (Algerian ivy), has very large, heart-shaped, glossy leaves and is a vigorous grower that thrives indoors. It also comes in a variegated form called 'Gloire de Marengo' with creamy white edges around a gray and green center. This ivy is not as susceptible to many of the pests and problems as other houseplant ivies.

4a

4b

4c

Many houseplants called ivy are really not ivies at all. This group includes:

4a. Swedish ivy, the plectranthus varieties, is sometimes called creeping Charlie. This charming, creeping plant has fragrant, oval, scalloped leaves; it is usually grayish-green with creamy-white edges but comes in many other colors and combinations. Sometimes the mature leaves turn purplish-pink around the edges or underneath. The small, tubular flowers are white to pale mauve and bloom intermittently throughout the year. These plants tolerate much drier conditions than true ivies. See Polka-Dot Plant, number 3.

4b. Grape ivy, the cissus varieties, also called kangaroo vine. These use tendrils to climb, and their foliage resembles grape or oak leaves.

4c. Devil's ivy or pothos (Scindapsus aureus) is a close relative of the philodendron. These durable, thick, glossy-leafed plants are available in solid green or have leaves marked with yellow or white spots and streaks. The plant's climbing, trailing habit "grows like the devil," hence the nickname devil's ivy. These plants need warmer temperatures than true ivies.

5. Ivies are perfect for combination plantings and can be planted at the base of many larger potted plants to give a softer, more finished look. See arranging tip 11.

6. Cascading ivy will give an old-world feel to any interior. This large French urn spilling over with ivy adds a lush garden touch to this living room.

5

6

NAME: Jade plant, jade tree, money plant.
VARIETIES: This family has more than 300 species, but the Crassula ovata varieties are the most common.
SEASON: Available all year.
COLOR: Silvery green to deep rich green. The tips can develop a red edge in full light conditions. There is an uncommon variegated white-and-green jade plant and an even rarer gold variety called sunset. Mature plants bear clusters of white or pale pink flowers.
SCENT: The flowers are fragrant.
LIGHT: Bright light. See care tip 41. Jades like a rest period in winter, so move them to a more shaded location.
TEMPERATURE: Average temperatures. See care tip 55. Leaves will drop in warmer temperatures.
WATER: Jades are a type of succulent. See care tip 14. Water thoroughly and let them dry before the next watering. Root rot is very common with jades and is caused by overwatering. See care tip 21.
HUMIDITY: Low. Jades tolerate dry air.
FOOD: Feed once a month with a weak solution during the growing months and not at all during the winter months. See care tips 71 and 74a. Cactus food works best for jade plants.
SOIL: Jades have shallow roots and like to be pot-bound, so repot every few years in a shallow pot. See container tip 1. Use soil with good draining qualities, such as a cactus mix, or add sand to regular potting soil. See care tips 65 and 80–83.
PESTS AND PROBLEMS: Mealy bugs. See care tip 110.
TIP: Jades look best when their leaves are naturally glossy, and they like an occasional shower to remove dust. See care tip 92. Prune to a desired shape or to expose more of the trunklike stem. Healthy, new growth will emerge from the pruned areas.
MEANING: The Chinese believe the jade plant brings prosperity.
NOTE: Jades can live for many years; some are reported to be over 100 years old. They are easily propagated from a single leaf. See care tip 86. You may notice new growth at the soil level of established plants from leaves naturally dropping from the main plant.

1. Jade plants are treelike succulents with stout, branching limbs and plump, oval leaves. A healthy jade plant will have many full clusters of leaves and sturdy stems.

2. Striking red tips are common on the leaves if kept in bright light.

3. This unusual variegated variety is striped cream and green.

4. (opposite) Beautiful white or pale pink flowers will bloom in the fall after the plant reaches maturity, usually after ten years.

5. Relatives of the jade plant in the crassula family also make interesting houseplants and interior accents.

6. These Asian plants can accent a contemporary setting or add an appropriate touch to a traditional interior.

1

3a   3b

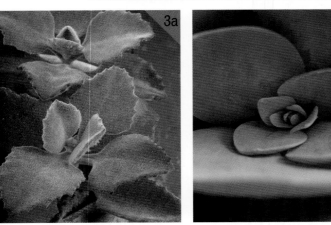

3c

NAME: Kalanchoe.

VARIETIES: Most common are the blossfeldiana hybrids, single and double varieties.

SEASON: Available all year.

COLOR: Red, yellow, orange, white, pinks, and magenta.

SCENT: None.

LIGHT: Bright light. See care tip 41. Kalanchoes in full bloom can be moved to lower light so the blooms will last longer, but low light can cause bud drop during the developing stage.

TEMPERATURE: Average temperatures. See care tip 55.

WATER: Although a succulent, kalanchoe requires more water than other succulents since it is also a flowering plant. See care tip 14. Plants kept too dry result in bud drop.

HUMIDITY: Low.

FOOD: Feed every two weeks while flowering with a mild solution. See care tip 74a and "Care after Flowering" below.

SOIL: Repot only when root-bound. See care tips 80–83. Use a lightweight potting soil with good draining qualities, a cactus mix, or mix sand into regular potting soil. See care tip 65.

PESTS AND PROBLEMS: Rare, but can attract scale, aphids, and mealy bugs. See care tip 110. Overwatering can cause mildew and stem rot.

NOTE: Kalanchoes are one of the few flowering plants that can tolerate dry winter heat indoors.

CARE AFTER FLOWERING: Trim spent flower stems to the second or third leaf below the stem. Let the plant rest in a cool spot with little water and no food for a couple of months. Three months before you want the plant to bloom, put the plant in complete darkness for twelve to sixteen hours each day. (Tip: Put a box over the plant.) After two months, increase the water. When new growth appears, feed with a weak solution every two weeks. When buds appear, after about a month, move the plant to normal light and continue to water and feed regularly.

1. Kalanchoes are cheerful plants with dark green leathery leaves and clusters of small tubular flowers. Buy kalanchoes with about one-third of their flowers open and with many healthy buds. Kalanchoes can last up to three months in bloom.

2. Flowering kalanchoes are a good choice for decorative plants at holiday time since they are abundant starting in fall. The red flowers are just as festive as traditional poinsettias and much easier to care for. The brilliant red is the perfect touch for this holiday table setting.

There are several nonflowering houseplant kalanchoes that are grown and appreciated for their unusual foliage. They get the same basic care as the flowering plants but require less water and food. See care tip 14.

3a. The felt plant (K. beharensis) has large serrated leaves that are covered with bronze hairs.

3b. K. thrysifolia is also called "flipping pancakes" for its rows of large, thick, round leaves.

3c. The panda plant (K. tomentosa) has velvety sage-green leaves trimmed in a deep brown.

NAME: Orchid.

VARIETIES: Orchids are the largest plant family with more than 25,000 species. Only a few are suitable as houseplants; these include phalaenopsis (moth orchid), paphiopedilum (lady's slipper orchid), and oncidium/odontoglossum (dancing lady orchid).

SEASON: All year.

COLOR: All colors, except true blue, in solid colors and mixes of patterns, stripes, and spots with every combination possible.

SCENT: Many varieties are fragrant.

LIGHT: Medium light in spring and summer and bright light in winter. See care tip 41. Orchids need ten to fifteen hours of light daily to ensure flower development. Leaves should be semi-erect and firm, not floppy or wilted. If leaves are too light, the plant is getting too much light; dark leaves indicate insufficient light. Buds that turn yellow, wilt, and fall before opening usually result from low light conditions.

TEMPERATURE: 70°F during the day, 10° to 15° cooler at night. See care tip 56. Avoid cold drafts.

WATER: Orchids need ample moisture and good drainage. In summer, water orchids every two or three days, once a week in winter. Always water orchids around the leaf base, soaking the roots and soil and allowing the plant to drain thoroughly. Do not let stand in water.

HUMIDITY: High. See care tips 31–37. When misting orchids, do not get water or moisture on the flowers, as brown specks on the petals and buds may result. Good ventilation and high humidity are essential. See care tip 51.

FOOD: Feed once a month with orchid food. See care tip 69. Small, yellow leaves and few flowers indicate a nutrient deficiency.

SOIL: Orchids like to be a little root-bound, so repot only when necessary, every two to three years, or when the potting media has decomposed. The best time to do this is in spring or summer. Remove the plant from its container and let the old mix fall away. Carefully trim away any old dead roots. Position the plant in its new container and pour in the new potting media, letting it settle around the roots. Use a coarse mix of bark chips or a mix designed specifically for orchids that will retain moisture and contain the right balance of nutrients. Orchid roots must be able to breathe, and regular potting soil will suffocate the roots. See care tips 80–83. Resume your normal watering and fertilizing schedule.

PESTS AND PROBLEMS: Rarely mealy bug and scale. See care tip 110. Mushy black spots on leaves indicate fungus. Remove these parts immediately and increase ventilation.

TIP: When orchids are not in flower, let them spend time outdoors in a warm, shady location. Bring the pots indoors in fall when temperatures begin to drop or when they are coming into flower. See care tip 54.

MEANING: "Beauty" or "You are a beautiful woman."

NOTE: Vanilla beans come from an orchid called Vanilla planifolla.

See following pages for captions.

Orchids are unique, captivating, powerful, mysterious, and drop-dead gorgeous. The most cherished plants in history, they have inspired works of art and literature. Today orchid growing is a huge industry and a passionate hobby for thousands of enthusiasts. The following are especially popular:

1a. Phalaenopsis: The moth orchid has large, flat-faced flowers with many blooms on long, arching stems. The leaves are rich green, wide, and strap-shaped with a leathery appearance. The name derives from the Greek words *phalaina* (moth) and *opsis* (similar to). It is not uncommon for flowers to last for three to five months, and you can often urge a second flowering with timely pruning. When the last flower of the spike fades, cut the spike one inch above the second node. If your plant is healthy and the season is not too late, this process will wake up one or two of the nodes and it may produce a new spray of fresh blooms in a few weeks.

1b. Paphiopedilum: The lady's slipper orchid has exotic, waxlike, richly colored blooms that can last for weeks. The name comes from the Greek word *pedilon* meaning sandal or slipper, a reference to the flower's large bulbous lower lip. Most plants have a single flower stem with one or two showy blossoms, often in outrageous colors. After flowering, the bloom will fade and fall off the plant. Snap the stem off near where it emerges from the plant to enable the orchid to use its energy to grow new roots and new growth for the next flowering. Lady slippers are very slow growers.

1c1 and 1c2. Oncidium/odontoglossum: Dancing lady orchids have pansylike blossoms that resemble delicate dancers in elaborate costumes (see also photo on page 129). The long, slender, branching sprays of many flowers come in vibrant, decorative colors and patterns. Many have a fragrance, including the most popular oncidium 'sharry baby' variety with its unique chocolate scent and the exotic odontoglossum brassia (spider orchid) varieties, which have a subtle vanilla and jasmine scent.

Two orchids commonly available as houseplants are very difficult to bring back into bloom under normal interior conditions, but they make wonderful temporary plants:

2a. Cymbidium.

2b. Dendrobium.

3. Orchids are now considered the most popular flowering houseplant and are often used instead of cut flowers to add a focal point to a room or interior setting. With their many varieties and diverse shapes and sizes, orchid flowers create a dramatic and long-lasting centerpiece of beautiful flowers that has endless possibilities. These white orchids add an unusual texture and beautiful softness to this traditional bedroom. See arranging tip 16.

1a

1b

2a

NAME: Palm.

VARIETIES: There are more than 3,000 species of palms, many of them suitable for houseplant use. Palms are generally divided into two botanical groups—the "feather" and the "fan" groups.

SEASON: Available all year.

COLOR: Shades of true green to deep green.

SCENT: None.

LIGHT: Bright light, but never direct sun. See care tip 41. Palms will also tolerate the lower light levels of most interior settings.

TEMPERATURE: Palms like warm summers, 70° to 80°F, and cooler winters, 50° to 60°F.

WATER: Keep evenly moist at all times. Do not water the heart of the plant, as this can cause root rot. Palms require good drainage, because their roots are sensitive to stagnant water. See care tips 8 and 22.

HUMIDITY: High. Mist palms once or twice a day to maintain humidity. Dry air may be the reason for brown leaf tips. See care tips 31–37.

FOOD: Feed with a very weak solution twice a month during the summer growing season and not at all during the winter months.

SOIL: Palms should be kept slightly root-bound, so they seldom need repotting. A deep pot is best, because most of the roots grow vertically. Palms do not like their roots disturbed, so do not trim or move the roots too much when repotting. See care tips 80–83. Make sure you use a good potting mix that retains moisture. The soil can be enhanced with sand for extra drainage, as this is how palms grow in nature.

PESTS AND PROBLEMS: Scale and red spider mites. See care tip 110.

TIP: The end of the stem where the fronds arise is the actively growing part of the plant. Give your palm plenty of room and do not touch or brush against it, as this will cause brown tips. Do not worry when an occasional leaf or two becomes discolored; this is part of the natural shedding process. Brown lower leaves are common and should be trimmed at once. Clean dusty foliage regularly with a damp cloth. See care tips 90 and 92.

MEANING: The palm is a Christian symbol for victory. The ashes used on Ash Wednesday are from burned palm leaves.

The feather palms have long fronds divided into many segments that resemble large feathers or fingers.

1a. The stately kentia palm (Howea forsteriana) has a slender trunk and gracefully arching fronds. The kentia takes four to seven years before it is ready to be sold and as a result, is quite expensive. It tolerates the lower light of most homes better than other palms.

1b. The areca or butterfly palm (Chrysalidocarpus lutescens), is one of the most graceful palms with long, thin, draping leaves of a glossy dark olive-green color and canelike green stems ringed with gold like bamboo.

The leaves of the fan palms are shaped much like a hand with the fingers spread. Two very popular types are:

2a. The lady palm (Rhapis excelsa) has dark green, glossy foliage with several leaflets on each frond and blunt tips. Lady palms are shaped more like shrubs than trees. This palm also comes in a variegated variety.

2b

3

4b

4a

5

2b. The Chinese fan, or fountain palm (Liveistona chinensis), has unusual fan-shaped foliage. Since its fronds can spread up to eight yards in diameter, the Chinese fan requires a lot of room. This palm also must have very bright light to survive.

3. Another very popular palm for indoor use is the fishtail palm (Caryota mitis). This is the only palm with leaves that are subdivided twice. The large split leaves have individual leaflets, which are triangular with a wavy edge. They look very much like fishtails.

Two other types of popular "palms" are not palms at all:

4a. The ponytail palm (Beaucarnea recurvata) is actually a type of succulent. See care tip 14. The swollen base of the trunk resembles an elephant's foot, which it is sometimes called. The trunk stores the water for the plant. The grassy arching leaves resemble a palm tree.

4b. The sago palm (Cycas revoluta) is an ancient plant species that dates back to the age of the dinosaurs. It has a unique pineapple-like trunk with brown scales and long, stiff, arching palm fronds emerging from the center. This plant is extremely slow-growing and may produce only a couple of leaves a year.

5. A graceful palm can add a soothing tropical touch to any setting. This large palm complements a rustic western interior with its arching greenery.

NAME: Peace lily, spathiphyllum, spathe.

VARIETIES: Of more than 35 species, Spathiphyllum clevelandii, S. floribundum, and S. wallisii are the most common houseplants, but hundreds of varieties are available, from delicate-leafed plants to those with giant elongated leaves.

SEASON: Available all year.

COLOR: Dark green, glossy foliage with white flowers. A variegated variety is also available.

SCENT: Flowers can be slightly fragrant.

LIGHT: Medium to bright light, but will survive in low light. See care tip 41. Keep out of direct sun, as leaves will yellow and the plant will not flower if it is in too bright a location.

TEMPERATURE: Between 70° and 80°F during the day with a ten-degree drop at night. Avoid drafts and temperatures below 60°. See care tip 53.

WATER: Moist at all times. They consume lots of water, so check two to three times a week. Leaves droop when the plant needs water. Peace lilies are very sensitive to tap water. See care tips 8, 16–18, and 26. Water less frequently in winter.

HUMIDITY: High. Brown leaf tips can result from low humidity. See care tips 31–37.

FOOD: Feed every two to three months, using a diluted solution of well-balanced liquid food. See care tip 70. Overfertilizing can cause brown leaf tips.

SOIL: Repot every year in spring. Use a soil mixture containing peat moss, because this is a bog plant requiring a reliably moist, acidic environment. See care tips 80–83. Sometimes these plants can double in size in one growing season. They are easily propagated by division. See care tip 84.

PESTS AND PROBLEMS: Mealy bugs and scale. See care tip 110.

TIP: Brown leaf tips are very common and can be caused by lack of humidity, over-feeding, or the use of tap water. Always trim off damaged leaves and spent flowers. Peace lilies have wide leaves that accumulate dust, so clean regularly. See care tips 90–93.

MEANING: The name peace lily was given to the plant because its flowers resemble the universally acknowledged white flag of truce. It is also a popular plant at times of bereavement.

NOTE: Rated as one of the top ten pollution fighters for interiors but are poisonous. See care tip 6.

1. Peace lilies have tufts of lush, glossy, dark green foliage and striking white flowers. Leaves should be sturdy and upright with good color.

2. The unusual variegated variety with textured foliage.

3. Because this is a sturdy plant that tolerates low-light conditions, the peace lily can bring elegance and beauty to any corner of a room with its stark white flowers against the deep emerald-green foliage.

4. (opposite) These beautiful and unusual flowers start out pale green and turn creamy white as they open. The large white "petal" is actually a spathe, or bract, which encloses the spike of tiny flowers. Peace lilies are one of the few foliage plants that will flower in low-light conditions.

NAME: Peperomia.

VARIETIES: There are more than 1,000 species of peperomias, which come in trailing, bushy, and upright varieties. The bushy varieties are those most commonly grown as houseplants.

SEASON: Available all year.

COLOR: Many shades of green and gray with stripes, marbled designs, or borders with contrasting colors of pale green, white, or silver.

SCENT: None, but a few rare varieties produce fragrant flowers.

LIGHT: Bright light without direct sun. See care tip 41. This plant will tolerate low light levels for extended periods of time.

TEMPERATURE: Between 55° and 85°F.

WATER: Plants can be watered from below. See care tip 20. Allow plants to dry slightly before watering. The succulent-like leaves and stems let them withstand short periods of drought.

HUMIDITY: High. See care tips 31–37, but do not mist these plants, because excess water and moisture lodged in the crevices of the textured leaves will cause rot.

FOOD: Plants should be fertilized twice a month in spring and summer with a diluted solution and not at all during the winter months.

SOIL: Peperomias do not need repotting often, only every few years or so. The plant is slow growing and prefers its roots in a pot that is a little on the small side. Peperomias require air around their roots, so use a very porous soil; heavy soil will suffocate this plant. The best soil mixture is one with a peat-moss base, or you may use standard potting soil and mix in one part sand. See care tips 80–83.

PESTS AND PROBLEMS: The most common problem is root rot caused by overwatering. See care tip 21. Mealy bugs and scale can also infest plants. See care tip 110.

TIP: Prune by pinching out spent or dead leaves to keep the plant looking attractive and to encourage more growth.

NOTE: Peperomias are related to the plant that produces the black pepper we use for seasoning.

Peperomias have highly ornamental foliage in a wide range of colors, textures, and leaf shapes, ranging from thread-like to heart-shaped. The foliage may be fleshy, corrugated, smooth, fuzzy, variegated, or even striped like a watermelon. Plants will produce long flower spikes throughout the year with tiny yellow, white, or pale green blossoms. P. argyreia, or the watermelon peperomia (opposite), has round, thick, deep green leaves with a swirly pale gray pattern resembling watermelon rind.

1a. Peperomia capreata, sometimes called emerald ripples, has thick heart-shaped, waxy, dark green leaves. The flowers are spikes of creamy white flowers.

1b. P. hederaefolia has metallic greenish-silver leaves and pale green flower spikes.

2. P. magnoliaefolia is the most common upright type for houseplant use. This peperomia resembles a jade plant with creamy variegated succulent leaves.

3. The striking metallic silver color of P. hederaefolia sets just the right tone for this formal table setting.

NAME: Philodendron, heart leaf.

VARIETIES: Many of the 300 species are suitable as houseplants. Philodendrons are categorized as either climbers or upright nonclimbers.

SEASON: Available all year.

COLOR: Shades of green, ranging from a true green to almost black. Some varieties have deep red accents or are variegated with cream splotches and stripes. The leaves of some hybrids range from pumpkin orange and pink to burgundy.

SCENT: None.

LIGHT: Medium light. See care tip 41. Some varieties can tolerate low-light conditions; those with unusual leaves need more light to keep their shape and color.

TEMPERATURE: Average temperatures. See care tips 55–57. Philodendrons do not like cold.

WATER: Water regularly, but allow the soil to dry slightly before watering. In winter, water sparingly, just enough to prevent drying out. Philodendrons are prone to root rot in winter if overwatered. See care tips 8 and 21.

HUMIDITY: Medium to high. See care tips 31–37.

FOOD: Feed monthly during the growing season but not in winter. To control growth, apply a fertilizer low in nitrogen once in spring and again in late summer. See care tip 70.

SOIL: Any houseplant potting soil is fine. Philodendrons need repotting only every three years or so. See care tips 80–83.

PESTS AND PROBLEMS: Mealy bugs and scale. See care tip 110.

TIP: Wash regularly as dust collects on the leaves and blocks pores. See care tips 89–92. The climbing varieties are typically displayed with a handmade pole, dried moss, and chicken wire, which create an unnatural appearance. Use an interesting branch instead to create a more natural presentation. See arranging tip 16.

NOTE: Philodendrons are very easy, tolerant houseplants, one of the best indoor pollution fighters. Some varieties are poisonous. See care tip 6.

MEANING: The name comes from the Greek, *philo* for love and *dendron* for tree. Philodendrons grow in the shadow of tall trees in the rain forest; the vine type climbs up trunks as high as 60 feet or more.

1. Philodendron leaves are traditionally heart shaped, but some resemble elephant ears, butterflies, or palm leaves. The vine type, such as the sweetheart variety, is the most common; its aggressive root system clings to everything and can easily reach the ceiling. Trim the roots to control growth.

2. The nonclimbing philodendrons have large leaves with deep scallops or lobes. As the plant ages, the leaves get bigger; a mature plant can reach seven to eight feet in all directions.

3. Monstera, or the Swiss cheese plant, is a close relative of the philodendron. In nature, the holes in the leaves let the rain through.

4a

4b

Hybrid upright philodendrons are available in striking colors:

4a. Moonlight glows in chartreuse green.

4b. Autumn in a rich pumpkin shade.

4c. Rich, deep burgundy variety.

5. Another close relative of the philodendron is the aglaonema, or Chinese evergreen plant. Aglaonemas have spear-shaped solid or showy variegated leaves. This plant requires the same care, but is very slow growing, much like the cast iron plant.

6. (opposite) Hybrid philodendrons are great accent plants with colorful foliage and low maintenance requirements. The brilliant green of the moonlight philodendron gives light and depth to this basket of jewel-tone lady's slipper orchids.

4c

5

NAME: Polka-dot plant, freckle face, hypoestes.
VARIETIES: Of the more than 100 closely related Hypoestes species, H. phyllostachya has the most common varieties for houseplant use.
SEASON: Available mostly in the spring and summer.
COLOR: Dark green foliage with pink, red, or white spotting.
SCENT: None.
LIGHT: Needs bright light. See care tip 41. Leaves will revert to green in lower light conditions and the plant gets spindly and weak.
TEMPERATURE: Average temperatures. See care tips 55–57. Plants cannot tolerate temperatures lower than 60°F.
WATER: Moist at all times. Water thoroughly and let become slightly dry before watering again. See care tip 21. Water more sparingly in winter.
HUMIDITY: High. See care tips 31–37.
FOOD: Feed once a month from spring through summer, not at all during the winter months.
SOIL: Repot every spring. Use any good house-plant potting soil; a potting mixture formulated for African violets is ideal. See care tips 80–83.
PESTS AND PROBLEMS: Aphids, mealy bugs, mites, and scale. See care tip 110. Rinse the foliage to clean the leaves and prevent pest infestations. See care tip 92.
TIP: Polka dots tend to get leggy with age, so keep them pinched back. See number 2 below. This plant won't be harmed at all if you feel the need to cut it back aggressively. In spring, insignificant small flowers appear and should be removed. See care tips 94 and 95.
NOTE: New plants are easy to propagate. Take tip cuttings and root them either in water or directly in soil. See care tips 86 and 87.

1. The polka-dot plant sounds like a party dress or hair ribbon, and it plays a similar fashion role in the plant world. This charming little plant is grown for its decorative foliage. The small ovate leaves are dark green with pink, red, or white polka dots.

2. The attractive colors and markings of the polka-dot plant make it a fun choice for mixed plantings. The white-spotted variety adds light and interest in this mixture of Swedish ivy.

3. The little polka-dot splashes will dress up and add a sweet touch to any area of your home.

NAME: Prayer plant.

VARIETIES: The marantha and calathea varieties are most commonly used as houseplants.

SEASON: Available all year.

COLOR: Striking foliage with contrasting color patches or stripes in all shades of green with touches of pink, red to burgundy, white, or cream.

SCENT: None.

LIGHT: Medium to bright light. See care tip 41. Direct light may cause leaf colors to fade; low light may cause colors to revert to solid green.

TEMPERATURE: Average temperatures. See care tips 55 –57. These plants like it fairly warm.

WATER: Moist at all times. Always use distilled or filtered water. See note below and care tips 16–18. Water sparingly in winter; brown streaks in foliage indicate too much water in cool conditions.

HUMIDITY: High. Mist a few times each day. Always double-pot these plants with moist moss. See care tips 31–37.

FOOD: Feed twice monthly spring to fall.

SOIL: Use a good potting mix without perlite, which contains fluoride. See "Pests and Problems" below. These plants have a shallow root system and need repotting every two to three years. See care tips 80–83 and container tip 1.

PESTS AND PROBLEMS: Spider mites. See care tip 110. Brown leaf tips are the most common problem, usually because of dry conditions or fluoride in the water or soil.

TIP: An occasional trim will encourage vigorous growth and help maintain a nice shape. The cut leaves will last for weeks in a vase and root easily in water. See care tip 87 and arranging tip 17.

MEANING: These plants fold up their leaves at night into a praying position.

1. (opposite) Prayer plants are striking houseplants, thanks to the elaborate markings on their leaves. A healthy plant should have richly colored leaves with no yellow or brown tips and with tightly furled new leaves. Small flowers may bloom in spring but are best trimmed away.

2a. The marantha varieties are the most common prayer plants: Marantha erythroneura, sometimes called the herringbone plant, with two-toned leaves of apple and emerald green accented with red veins and deep burgundy undersides.

2b. M. kerchoviana, or rabbit tracks, has evenly spaced dark patches like the tracks of a rabbit.

3a. The calatheas are the showiest of the group of prayer plants. Calathea roseopicta has olive green leaves with a light-colored feather pattern accented with deep burgundy.

3b. C. makoyana is also called the peacock plant because of its ornate pattern.

4. Prayer plants with their many patterns and details look great in a setting with a similar feel. Plants such as C. lubbersii, mix well with rich jewel-tone fabrics and textures.

NAME: Snake plant, mother-in-law tongue, sansevieria.

VARIETIES: There are more than 30 varieties, but the most common houseplant is the Sansevieria trifasciata Laurentii.

SEASON: Available all year.

COLOR: Variations of green with striations through the foliage of dark green, gold, white and silver.

SCENT: The rare flowers are fragrant.

LIGHT: Medium to bright light. See care tip 41. Snake plants can tolerate a wide range of light conditions, but good light keeps the beautiful markings on the leaves and low light may cause the leaves to lose colors and revert to solid green.

TEMPERATURE: Average temperatures, but the plant prefers warmth. See care tips 55–57.

WATER: Classified as a succulent. See care tip 14. Water every other week during the growing season and very sparingly during winter—just enough to prevent plant from completely drying out. If leaves collapse, the plant has been over-watered.

HUMIDITY: Low.

FOOD: Feed once a year at the beginning of the growing season in spring.

SOIL: Very slow-growing; usually needs repotting every three to four years. Use a porous potting mix formulated for succulents or a mix of equal parts potting soil, peat moss, and sand. See care tips 65 and 80–85. Plants must be pot-bound to flower.

PESTS AND PROBLEMS: Mealy bugs. See care tip 110.

TIP: This plant may be slow-growing but is very durable, sometimes called the black thumb's plant. Keep leaves groomed, as they easily gather dust and have a dull appearance. If leaf tips are damaged, the plant will stop growing. If a leaf is damaged or flops over, cut it off at the base and a new leaf will emerge.

MEANING: This plant gets its name mother-in-law tongue from the long tonguelike leaves with sharp tips. The Chinese treasure this plant because they believe it bestows eight great gifts—long life, prosperity, intelligence, beauty, art, poetry, health, and strength.

NOTE: This plant is a great pollution fighter but is poisonous. See care tip 6.

1. (opposite) Snake plants have long, stiff, upright leaves with contrasting stripes and bands. The leaf markings resemble snake skin, hence its common name. Plants can reach to five feet or more.

2. The hahnii variety, or the bird's-nest sansevieria, is a low-growing plant with a rosette of marbled leaves.

3. Snake plants may flower in the right conditions. The flowers are pale green and fragrant.

4. These plants can be very showy when displayed in a row, like a hedge. The long bladelike leaves make a great dividing wall or addition to a large space when massed together or a perfect summer decoration for a fireplace, as the foliage fills the space with cool green flames.

NAME: Spider plant, ribbon plant, chlorophytum.
VARIETY: Chlorophytum comosum.
SEASON: Available all year.
COLOR: Most have variegated green-and-white or green-and-yellow striped foliage. There is also a solid green variety, but it is rarely available as a houseplant.
SCENT: None.
LIGHT: Bright, filtered light; will survive in lower light conditions but growth will not be as vigorous. See care tip 41.
TEMPERATURE: Average temperatures, but can withstand colder or warmer conditions. See care tip 55.
WATER: This plant can be watered thoroughly, but allow it to dry out before watering. See care tips 21 and 22. Spider plants are native to hot, dry climates and have thick, fleshy roots that store water. Water sparingly during the winter. Brown streaks in the foliage during winter indicate too much water in cool conditions.
HUMIDITY: Medium to high. See care tips 31–37. Brown tips are a common problem, caused by a lack of humidity or from the type of soil mix. Frequent misting is helpful. See "Soil" below.
FOOD: Feed twice a month during growing season, March to August, and not at all during the winter months.
SOIL: Use a mixture without perlite, which contains fluoride that can cause brown leaf tips. Do not repot often, as the plant's roots must fill the pot before it produces plantlets. A mass of plantlets indicates the need for repotting, probably every two years. See care tip 83.
PESTS AND PROBLEMS: Rare.
TIP: When brown leaf tips occur, trim the damaged leaves back to the base and increase humidity.
NOTE: Spider plants are one of the best indoor pollution fighters.

1. (opposite) The long, arching foliage usually has several dangling plantlets that resemble spiders on a web.

2. The solid-green spider plant is less common than the striped varieties.

3. When the plantlets are trimmed away, a spider plant can be used as an upright plant and grouped with other plants to create a woodland look. Here the striped ribbon foliage complements the flowering bulbs, adding a grassy element.

4. The grassy spider plant foliage also mixes well with the lacy texture of ferns, and both will benefit from extra humidity.

5. Spider plants are one of the easiest plants to propagate. Place a plantlet on top of a small pot of potting mix while the stem is still attached to the mother plant, and secure it with a bent wire. Once the plantlet establishes roots, cut it away from the mother plant.

NAME: String of hearts, hearts entangled, rosary vine.

VARIETIES: Ceropegia woodii.

SEASON: Available all year.

COLOR: Silvery green heart-shaped leaves with small tubular pale pink flowers.

SCENT: None.

LIGHT: Bright. See care tip 41. Some direct sun during the day for a few hours is fine.

TEMPERATURE: Likes average to slightly warmer temperatures. See care tips 55–57.

WATER: Classified as a succulent. See care tip 14. Plants should be thoroughly watered and then allowed to dry before the next watering. In winter, water just enough to prevent the plant from drying out completely.

HUMIDITY: Low.

FOOD: Feed once a month with a very weak solution during the growing months and not at all during the winter.

SOIL: Repot every two or three years. Use a potting mix formulated for succulents or cacti or mix equal parts sand into the potting soil. See care tip 65.

PESTS AND PROBLEMS: Mealy bugs. See care tip 110.

TIP: These plants thrive in warm and dry conditions, and their minimal need for water makes them an ideal choice for high-placed trailing plants. Plants can become leggy and straggly over time, and it is best to cut back the vines to a few inches and wait for new growth.

MEANING: This plant is symbolic of love because the leaves are entangled just like the hearts of lovers.

NOTE: String of hearts is a perfect romantic gift, as the name implies. This beautiful, delicate vine will last longer than traditional red roses.

1. (opposite) String of hearts is a delicate trailing plant that can grow to several feet long. The heart-shaped leaves have beautiful silver markings and very small, pale pink, tubular flowers. The leaves should be plump and the top of the plant should have good, healthy coverage of foliage and vines at soil level.

2. The pea-size roots are storage vessels for water and food. Smaller beadlike roots will develop along the stems (hence the nickname "rosary vine"); these are young seed vessels that can be easily rooted to make new plants or fuller plants. Push these seed pods down into the soil and wait for new growth.

3. Another similar succulent vine is the string of beads or string of pearls, which has green trailing stems and small fragrant flowers at the base of the plant.

4. The delicate vines give a soft accent with just the right touch without overpowering a space like traditional larger leaf vines. The heart leaves look dainty dangling down the side of this primitive urn without covering the beautiful color and detail of the container.

NAME: Syngonium, nephthytis, arrowhead vine, white butterfly vine.

VARIETIES: There are 33 species of syngoniums. The most common and popular species for a houseplant is Syngonium podophyllum, whose varieties are available in large and dwarf types.

SEASON: Available all year.

COLOR: Bright green leaves with silver, white, or yellow markings. Pink and bronze shades are also available.

SCENT: None.

LIGHT: Bright to medium light, but no direct sun, as the leaves will easily scorch. See care tip 41. This plant will tolerate low light conditions for extended periods of time.

TEMPERATURE: Warm temperatures, 80 to 85°F during the day and about 65° at night.

WATER: Moist at all times. Water thoroughly and then allow the plant to dry slightly before the next watering. See care tips 21 and 22. Water more sparingly in winter.

HUMIDITY: Medium to high. Misting is good for this plant. See care tips 31–37.

FOOD: Feed every two weeks during the spring and summer growing season and not at all in winter.

SOIL: Repot every spring. Use any good houseplant potting mix. See care tips 80–83.

PESTS AND PROBLEMS: Scale, mites, and aphids. See care tip 110.

TIP: Prune occasionally to keep the plant under control and in its more attractive juvenile state. When the plant matures, provide a pole or branch for climbing and support. See its close relative the philodendron. See arranging tip 16.

MEANING: The name nephthytis is derived from Nephthys, the Egyptian goddess of households.

NOTE: All parts of the plant are poisonous. See care tip 6.

1. Syngoniums have big, soft, flowing leaves with intricate patterns and crisp colors. Some of this plant's common names refer to the shape of the leaves at different stages of development. The young leaves are shaped like arrows or butterflies, and at this attractive stage, the variegation is boldest and brightest. In time, dramatic changes in leaf shape will take place. The bold leaves begin to form lobes and become stiff-looking, and the stems acquire a climbing habit and start to vine.

2. When purchasing a plant, look for lots of new growth, which is indicated by many unfurling, bright green leaves, and a compact, full appearance.

3. Some varieties have subtle shades of bronze and pink and tend to remain more compact and bushlike longer than their green trailing cousins.

4. Syngoniums are handsome in hanging baskets and as large pot plants grown alone, but they also add interest to a mixed planting. Arrowhead plants are rapid growers and will spill out of a hanging basket or over a planter edge for a full, lush look. A big basket of white butterfly plants gives a light, summery, almost tropical feel to this setting.

NAME: Wandering Jew, tradescantia, inch plant.
VARIETIES: Tradescantia fluminensis varieties.
SEASON: Available all year, but more prominent in the spring and summer.
COLOR: Variegated foliage in shades of white, yellow, green, pink, purple, and silver. The inconspicuous flowers range from white to shades of pink.
SCENT: None.
LIGHT: Prefers bright to medium light, but avoid full sun. See care tip 41. If the variegation starts to fade, more light is needed.
TEMPERATURE: Average temperatures, but not below 55°F. See care tips 55–57.
WATER: Moist at all times. See care tips 21 and 22. Water less in winter.
HUMIDITY: Medium to high. See care tips 31–37.
FOOD: Feed every two weeks with a diluted solution in the growing months and not at all during the winter.
SOIL: Repot every spring in any good house-plant potting mix. See care tips 80–83.
PESTS AND PROBLEMS: Spider mites. See care tip 110.
TIP: Pinch plants occasionally to keep them bushy and full; see care tip 95. After a year or so, tradescantias usually become leggy and unhealthy. You can cut the old plant back to a few inches and let it rejuvenate, or start a new plant with tip cuttings. See care tip 87. These plants like to summer outside. See care tip 54.
MEANING: The "wandering Jew" is a figure from Christian folklore, a Jewish shoemaker who taunted Christ on the way to the crucifixion and was cursed by him to "go on forever till I return." The shoemaker was thus punished by being forced to wander the earth. This name was given to the tradescantia because of its wandering, spreading nature.

1. Wandering Jew, or tradescantia, is a lovely trailing plant with succulent-like, ovate, shimmering leaves that have a slightly puckered texture. Small three-petal flowers appear in clusters from spring through fall. The foliage is striped in cool shades of green and white or in combinations of burgundy, silver, and green. These plants are rapid growers.

2a. The bridal veil plant has small, glossy, deep-green foliage covered with many tiny white flowers.

2b. The closely related Bolivian Jew variety, or turtle vine, has tiny ovate leaves and is more clumplike in growth.

3. Wandering Jew makes a wonderful houseplant that can be used in a variety of ways. Its cascading nature and interesting variegations make a striking hanging basket and add texture to mixed plantings. These plants can also be used to finish the base of many larger pot plants. See Ivy, number 5.

NAME: Zebra plant.

VARIETY: Aphelandra squarrosa.

SEASON: Available all year.

COLOR: Deep green ovate leaves with white or silver striping. In late summer to early fall, golden yellow flower spikes may appear.

SCENT: None.

LIGHT: Bright light, but no direct sun. See care tip 41. For zebra plants to bloom, they must be in a well-lit area. Lower light conditions will produce only leaves.

TEMPERATURE: Prefers warm temperatures during the growing months, about 80°F; after the plant flowers, it prefers cooler temperatures, about 60°. This plant does not tolerate temperatures below 55° or cold drafts.

WATER: Moist at all times. Zebra plants must never be allowed to dry out. Even a short period of drought can cause severe leaf loss. See care tips 21 and 22. Zebra plants drop leaves from both overwatering and underwatering. Less water is needed after flowering and in the winter months.

HUMIDITY: High. Brown leaf tips are common. See care tips 31–37.

FOOD: Feed twice a week with a diluted solution during the growing season, from spring to fall, when flowering is common, and not at all during winter.

SOIL: Use a nutrient-rich potting mix that drains well. Zebra plants should be repotted in the spring. See care tips 80–83.

PESTS AND PROBLEMS: Aphids, spider mites, mealy bugs, and scale. See care tip 110. Excess water on the leaves can result in mold.

TIP: Zebra plants tend to get leggy, so pinch the growing tips from time to time to keep the plant full and bushy. See care tip 95. It is common for the lower leaves to fall off the plant from under- or overwatering or as the plant gets older.

1. The zebra plant gets its name from the dramatic stripes on its large, dark green leaves.

2. This plant is handsome because of its foliage, but in optimal conditions it will also send out beautiful yellow flower spikes. Prune back the flower stalk once the flowers fade. Zebra plants need a winter rest period to flower again the next year.

3. The zebra plant adds an exotic touch to any interior. The animal-print leaves offset green-and-white lady's slipper orchids in this striking planter combination.

Acknowledgments

Many thanks to Margaret Kaplan, who has given me two great opportunities at Abrams, who believed in my work from the beginning, and who always remained thoughtful and encouraging along the way.

I would also like to thank the others who helped in so many ways to bring this book together: Robin and Bill Weiss; Jeanne Maher; Pat and Bill Wilson; Gary, Barbara, and Glenn Ronning; Ann and Allen Dick; Kathy and Lee Gardner; Dominique Yvernault; Christian Burch; and Kelly and Lee Beaman.

Thanks as well to Barbara Burn, Darilyn Carnes, and Harriet Whelchel at Abrams for all of their hard work and patience with this project and for creating a beautiful book.

My gratitude also goes to T.K. Hill for the many hours he spent photographing houseplants with me.

I am grateful to Claudia Dragonette, Shila Dalebout, Courtney Askew, and Maura Kearney for their care of many houseplants during the past few years.

A special thank-you goes to my mother for the memories I have of the many beautiful plants in our house, especially the two giant ferns.

And, as always, thank you, Vincent.

Editor:
Barbara Burn

Editorial Assistant:
Jon Cipriaso

Designer:
Darilyn Lowe Carnes

Production Manager:
Jane Searle

Library of Congress Cataloging-in-Publication Data

Heffernan, Cecelia.
  Houseplants A to Z : buying, growing, arranging /
Cecelia Heffernan ; photography by T. K. Hill.
    p. cm.
  Includes bibliographical references and index.
  ISBN 0–8109–5544–X (hardcover : alk. paper) 1. Houseplants.
I. Title.

SB419.H394 2006
635.9'65—dc22

2005032510

Text copyright © 2006 Cecelia Heffernan
Illustrations/photographs copyright © 2006 T. K. Hill

Published in 2006 by Abrams, an imprint of Harry N. Abrams, Inc.
All rights reserved. No portion of this book may be reproduced,
stored in a retrieval system, or transmitted in any form or by
any means, mechanical, electronic, photocopying, recording,
or otherwise, without written permission from the publisher.

Printed and bound in Singapore

10 9 8 7 6 5 4 3 2 1

HNA ▪▪▪▪▪
harry n. abrams, inc.
a subsidiary of La Martinière Groupe
115 West 18th Street
New York, NY 10011
www.hnabooks.com